CINEMA OF MYSTERY

Arthur Rackham illustrated the tale of Edgar Allan Poe most often made into a film – *The Murders in the Rue Morgue.*

CINEMA OF MYSTERY
by Rose London

Bounty Books

Copyright © MCMLXXV by Lorrimer Publishing Ltd.
Library of Congress Catalog Card Number: 75-37326
All rights reserved.
This edition is published by Bounty Books
a division of Crown Publishers, Inc.
by arrangement with Lorrimer Publishing Ltd.
a b c d e f g h
Manufactured in the United States of America

Designed by Dave Allen
Cover designed by JWA Designs

Contents

The publishers wish to acknowledge their debt to the following people and organisations: Edgar Allan Poe, Aubrey Beardsley, Arthur Rackham, W. Heath Robinson, the British Film Institute, 20th Century Fox, MGM-EMI, Columbia-Warner, United Artists, Allied Artists, Paramount, Universal MCA, RCO General Inc., Rank, First National Cinema International Corporation, Hammer, the Cinema Bookshop, Anglo-Amalgamated, AIP, Contemporary Films, British Lion, Hemdale, Intercontinental Films, the stills and information departments of the National Film Archives, Titan International, Don Getz, Al Reuter, Brian McIlmail, Martin Jones and with special thanks to: Boris Karloff, Bela Lugosi, Vincent Price, Peter Lorre, and Roger Corman.

Quoth the Raven, Evermore

'My God, she is dead!'
From D. W. Griffith's Edgar Allan Poe *(1909)*

Half a century before the cinema of mystery was invented, Edgar Allan Poe had already imagined its themes and written its treatments. In France, the brothers Lumière discovered the technique and Méliès the magic of the new medium that Hollywood was to exploit. In the same way, France had discovered the gothic and tragic genius of Poe; he was translated by Baudelaire and became a major influence on French literature before America recognised later the tormented master whom it had ignored. Just as the whole cinema of the monster and the vampire derives from the gothic conversations of Byron and the Shelleys round Lake Geneva in 1816 – resulting in the writing of 'Frankenstein' and the fragment called 'The Vampire' – so most of our cinema of mystery and detection comes from Poe's 'Tales of the Grotesque and Arabesque', first published in 1840, and later republished often under the title of 'Tales of Mystery and Imagination'.

From the tortured imaginings of that obsessed orphan, half-mad with opium and alcohol and failure and ill-health, sprang the themes that haunt our eyes today – the themes of death and the undead of 'The Black Cat' and 'The Premature Burial', the themes of plague and ruin of 'The Masque of the Red Death' and 'The Fall of the House of Usher', the themes of torture and revenge of 'The Pit and the Pendulum' and 'The Cask of Amontillado', the themes of retribution and remorse of 'William Wilson' and 'The Tell-Tale Heart'.

When we add to these themes Poe's creation of the method of the detective story in 'The Murders in the Rue Morgue' and 'The Mystery of Marie Rogêt', we realise that Poe originated the cinema of suspense single-handed. His sleuth, C. Auguste Dupin, makes the Hercule Poirot of *Murder on the Orient Express* seem like a schoolboy at the master's desk. As Howard Haycraft has written in his excellent *Murder for Pleasure:* 'The transcendent and eccentric detective; the admiring and slightly stupid foil; the well-intentioned blundering and unimaginativeness of the official guardians of the law; the locked-room convention; the pointing finger of unjust suspicion; the solution by surprise; deduction by putting one's self in another's position (now called psychology); concealment by means of the ultra-obvious; the staged ruse to force the culprit's hand; even the expansive and condescending explanation when the chase is done; all these sprang full-panoplied from the buzzing brain and lofty brow of the Philadelphia editor . . . Nothing really primary has been added either to the framework of the detective story or to its internals since Poe.'

Such a talent for imagination and origination sparked off an interest in the man himself. He was born in 1809, the third child of travelling actors. His elder brother was to die of drink, his sister was subnormal. He was adopted by an unloving and stern foster-father, who brought him up to be a gentleman in Richmond, Virginia, then cut him off without a penny to scribble in poverty. He enlisted anonymously in the US Army, rose to be a Sergeant Major, left the Army, re-enlisted again to become an officer at West Point, then finally quit. He loved his aunt, Mrs Maria Clemm and married her daughter and his cousin Virginia when she was only thirteen. Perhaps the marriage was never consummated, for she was his pure and distant fantasy woman among

POE'S TALES
OF MYSTERY & IMAGINATION
ILLUSTRATED BY
ARTHUR RACKHAM

Aubrey Beardsley did four illustrations of Poe's stories. Here is his picture for the decadent orgy in 'The Masque of the Red Death.'

Left: This is Arthur Rackham's cover for an edition of Poe's stories published in 1935.

THE NIGHT'S   PLUTONIAN SHORE

This illustration of 'The Raven' was done by the young W. Heath Robinson in 1900, at a time when he was much under Beardsley's influence.

others, his Lenore, his Ligeia, his death-in-life woman, who slowly died before his eyes of a series of broken blood-vessels. Failing as a writer and editor, penniless and driven by dreams and opium, Poe fell to pieces at the end of his life and died in 1849, ruined in body and career. Death was to love this man in love with death. His own burial would prove premature, for his writings were to rise from his grave to speak to us all.

The first great director of the new cinema, D. W. Griffith, took Poe himself as the subject of a one-reel film in 1909, on

A startling German postcard of 1900, obviously influenced by Poe, has the birds of death perched on the dream body of love.

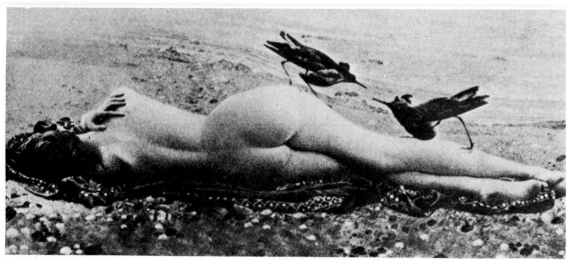

the centenary of the writer's birth. It was a genre called a 'biopic' made for the Mutoscope and Biograph Company and it was called *Edgar Allan Poe*. Herbert Yost played Poe himself and Griffith's actress wife played Virginia Clemm. Always in love with the melodrama of history, Griffith chose to treat Poe's most famous poem 'The Raven' as a matter of fact. So the film opens with Poe looking after his dying wife and opening a window. At that moment, a raven flies in and sits on 'the pallid bust of Pallas just above his chamber door'. Inspiration comes on instant black wings to Edgar and he dashes off his poem 'The Raven' and pelts out to sell it. Spurned by one editor, he finds another who gives him ten dollars for his masterpiece. He buys medicine and food and a wrap for Virginia, but when he gets back home, she is cold and still, and he falls across her sick-bed with the printed title, 'My God, she is dead!' The omen of the bird of death has taken with it his wife's soul back to the Night's Plutonian shore.

Griffith's film was successful enough for the American Eclair Company to make *The Raven* in 1912, another two-reel film about Poe, which featured some of his more famous tales. In this version, Guy Oliver played Poe, closely resembling him in his lanky looks, and there were location shots of the actual Poe cottage at Fordham. Again the writer tries to look after his invalid wife, here called Lenore instead of Virginia after 'the lost Lenore' of Poe's poem. He falls asleep and dreams up scenes from 'The Pit and the Pendulum', 'The Black Cat', 'The Murders in the Rue Morgue', and more of his stories. Waking, he finds himself in a well-appointed study, writing the poem of 'The Raven'. The black bird taps at the window, and once again perches on the bust of Pallas and watches him write the poem. Copying Griffith's sequence, Poe rushes out to sell the poem and comes back with food and medicine. But the ending is less bleak – Lenore is still alive when he returns.

D. W. Griffith returned to his fascination with Poe in 1914 with possibly the best adaptation ever made of the Poe material. He had discovered an actor, Henry B. Walthall, who had a similar appearance to Poe and a gift for emulating the writer's habits. Now exploiting Walthall's resemblance to Poe, Griffith's film, *The Avenging Conscience,* and Charles J. Brabin's remake of *The Raven* in 1915 used the same shot to establish the similarity of Walthall and Poe, a direct cut from an authentic Poe portrait (autographed Edgar A. Poe) to a medium close-up of Walthall framed like the portrait. The Griffith's film of Walthall as Poe was not a 'biopic' this time, but a version of 'The Tell-Tale Heart', in which Walthall is an orphan, whose guardian and uncle is trying to break up his romance with the local belle, just like Poe's foster-father Allan had helped to break up his first romance with Sarah Elmira Royster. Walthall is actually reading Poe's tales of terror and is inspired by 'The Tell-Tale Heart' to kill his uncle and put his body behind the wall. As in Poe's story, the young murderer loses his head under investigation, because of the monotonous sequence of an owl hooting, intercut with the movement of a pendulum swinging, and the tapping of the detective's foot and pencil. But as he confesses, he wakes to find the whole murder a recorded hallucination – as it was for Poe.

A vision of Christ appears to Walthall, the murderer, in *The Avenging Conscience* (1914).

Walthall, here seen with Rafaela Ottiana and the miniature Grace Ford, remained as an actor in macabre movies – in this case in Tod Browning's *Devil Doll* (1936).

Brabin's film with Walthall, however, was based on a book and a play about the Irish and Virginian ancestors of the writer. It establishes Poe as the heir of the American revolutionary tradition, but once again the film concentrates on the writing of 'The Raven' and the death of Poe 's young wife. The film cheats in making Walthall die himself after completing 'The Raven', but is otherwise distinguished only for Walthall's *doppelganger* of a performance. The backers, the Essanay Company, even called Walthall the 'image of Poe' and 'a man of the same mould and temperament'.

This film ended for twenty-seven years the use of Poe himself in the material he invented. There were to be two other full-scale versions of his life, 20th Century Fox's *The Loves of Edgar Allan Poe* of 1942 and MGM's *The Man with a Cloak* of 1951. In the first of these, John Shepperd played Poe indifferently; in the second, Joseph Cotten played him sombrely, rather in the manner of his role as Holly Martins in *The Third Man*. The plot of the 1942 film was overblown and romantic, but the 1951 version had Leslie Caron come to New York to persuade her paralysed and drunken grandfather, played by Louis Calhern, to change his will in her lover's favour. She is befriended by a mysterious Man with a Cloak, who happens to quote poetry, answers to the name of 'Dupin', and is

Dr Diabolo brings in the crowd to his Torture Garden – films themselves were first shown in fairgrounds.

followed by a raven. No names, but strong hints.

The most recent time Poe has surfaced as a spooky character in his own right is in Antonio Margheriti's *La Danza Macabra* of 1963, where the drunken Poe introduces the story of Berenice in an Usher-like haunted castle, and in· the Amicus production of *The Torture Garden* of 1966. This haunting movie begins with a Dr. Diabolo, who runs a fairground show like Dr. Caligari, proposing to five visitors that he should reveal to them their future. A woman representing Atropos, the Goddess of Destiny, cuts the thread of each of their lives. In an echo of Poe, Colin, the society boy, is pushed by his greed to death at the claws of a homicidal cat. And in the final episode a passionate collector of the works of Poe reveals that Poe himself comes back from the dead to write new manuscripts for him. Now the writer is his own ghost, manufacturing dreams . . .

If the early American cinema concentrated on Poe, the man of spirit, the early German cinema concentrated on one of his stories, the somewhat autobiographical

Atropos cuts the thread of Michael Bryant's life in *The Torture Garden* (1966).

William Wilson, because its theme was Germanic, that of the *doppelganger*. Paul Wegener's *The Student of Prague* of 1913 used the theme of the evil double from 'William Wilson' mixed with Hoffman's ideas of malicious replicas of oneself and with the legend of Faust. Wegener's version (and a later one by Henrik Galeen in 1926 starring Conrad Veidt) both used Poe's idea of the identical student with the same birth-date mimicking his double; but they had to add a Mephisto or Caligari-type of

Hedger Wallace plays the resurrected Poe in *The Torture Garden*.

Rackham's version of William Wilson confronting his double.

sorcerer to perform the trick of the split self, instead of leaving it to the hallucination of conscience as in the Poe version. At any rate, it provided a good occasion for the demonstration of early split-screen techniques and catered to the German sense of the schizoid personality.

Half a century later, Louis Malle was to remake 'William Wilson' starring Alain Delon and Brigitte Bardot, as one of three

episodes (with Fellini and Vadim) in AIP's *Spirits of the Dead* of 1969. Delon plays the split-minded Wilson with an elegance and a sadism that is true to the spirit of Poe. His breakdown into paranoia is believable and the story is told with economy. Unfortunately, the inclusion of Bardot, including a bare-backed whipping sequence, is superfluous and rather ridiculous, while some of the images of horror are more Hammer than Edgar – a scalpel in a corpse, the torture of a schoolboy by rats, and a knife-edge stroking a girl's face.

The early French cinema was less interested in Poe, the man of the split mind, than in Poe the story-teller. His huge influence on the Symbolist writers, owing to Baudelaire's advocacy, had inspired personally Mallarmé and Verlaine and Rimbaud, as well as a general appreciation of his gothic excess. Poe had also inspired some of the greatest English graphic artists to illustrate his works, particularly Aubrey Beardsley, W. Heath Robinson and Arthur Rackham. Both the shadowy symbolist writers and the swirling crochety demoniac English illustrators were picked up by the new European directors and art-designers to create a cinema of excess and eccentricity, trouble and devil, that owed much to the emanation of Poe from beyond the grave.

In the same centenary of Poe's birthday that Griffith made his 'biopic' of the writer, Henri Desfontaines made his first Poe story, *The Gold-Bug,* followed in 1910 by *Hop-Frog* and *The Pit and the Pendulum.* None of these early versions are viewable, while the Maurice Tourneur film of the Poe story in which the inmates take over the asylum, *The System of Dr. Goudron and Professor Plume,* is a rarity. In that film, which American Eclair issued under the title of *The Lunatics* in 1913, Henri Gouget played one of the mad scientists, based on Poe's 'Dr. Tarr and Professor Fether'. One of its images, that of blood oozing out from under a locked door, was to become a staple sight of the horror movie. But as for the actual depiction of scientific lunacy, it

Alain Delon plays William Wilson, here seen seducing Carla Marlier in *Spirits of the Dead*.

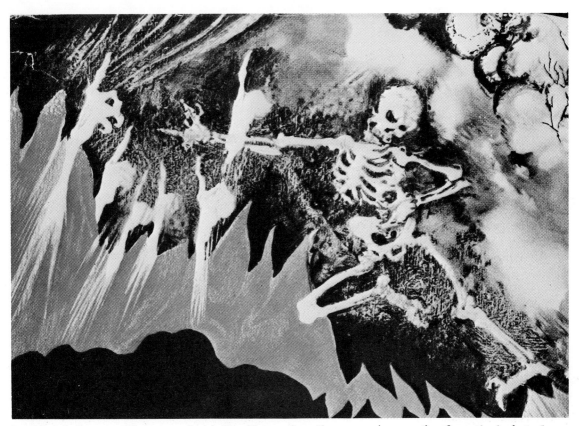

Rackham's finest work appears in his Poe illustrations, here seen in a section from the jacket of the book of Poe's Tales, and in an endpiece to one of the tales.

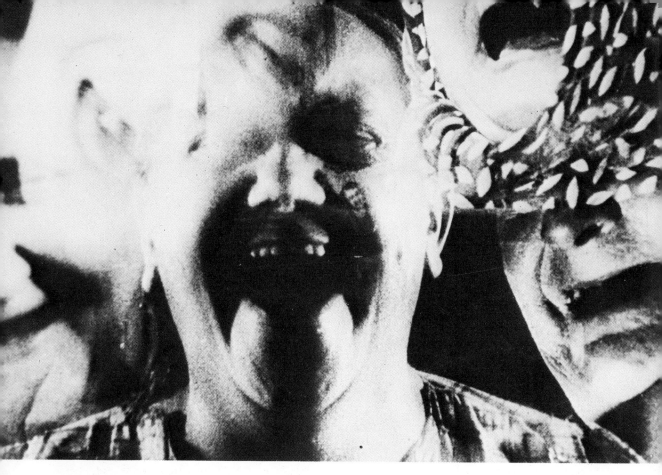

The Poe-inspired cinema of distortion pioneered by Gance was followed up by Murnau in *The Last Laugh* in 1925.

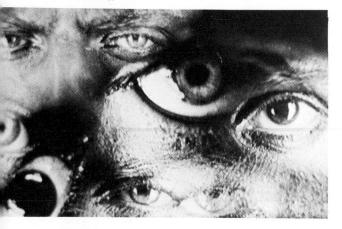

would take the genius of Abel Gance to show it in the distortions of his early work, *The Madness of Dr. Tube*.

The early Russian cinema is said by Jay Leyda in *Kino* to have produced two films derived from Poe, Twrzhansky's *Isle of Oblivion* of 1917 and Gardin's *A Spectre Haunts Europe* of 1923, based on 'The Masque of the Red Death'. But Stalin's iron hand on the Soviet cinema soon put a stop to such reveries. And the practicality of the early 1920s both in America and Europe, led Poe to be banished to the hands of the experimental film-makers, until the rise of the horror cult in the late twenties and early thirties led to his second great period of influence on the cinema.

Now that Poe has been introduced as a force in the origins of the cinema, his themes can be considered one by one. His first theme was his horror of living death and the undead memory of the dead, the theme of waking in a coffin, of corpses rising from the crypt, and of the possession of breathing women by their buried counterparts. As he wrote in 'The Premature Burial' of one of his own experiences:

The conclusion was irresistible. I was not within the vault. I had fallen into a trance while absent from home – while among strangers – when, or how, I could not remember – and it was they who had buried me as a dog – nailed up in some common coffin – and thrust, deep, deep, and forever, into some ordinary and nameless grave.

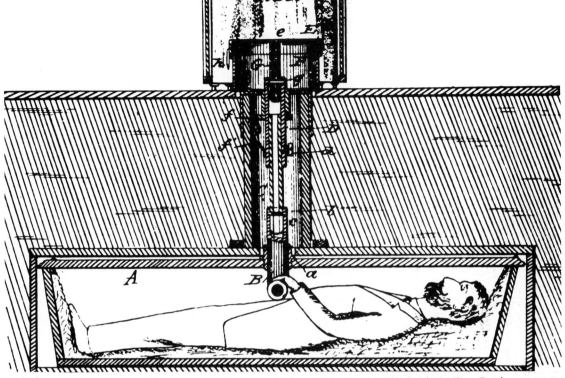

Statistically, it is estimated that one in five hundred people are actually buried alive. Poe's story of Premature Burial so horrified a German inventor, Krichbaum, that he recommended in 1882 the fitting of a pneumatic tube to every coffin, in case the corpse revived and needed to send a message to the living.

Krichbaum was followed by a Russian inventor in 1901 Count Karnice-Karnicky, who had seen a young Belgian girl wake from the dead as the first earth hit her coffin. He preferred a simpler system like a railway signal attached to the coffin of the dead-alive.

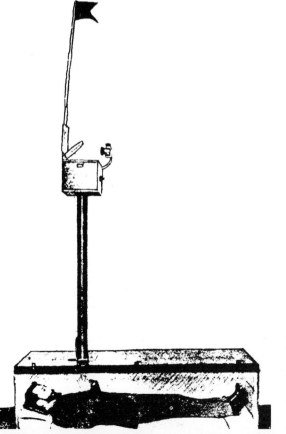

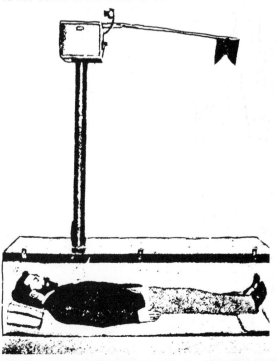

Rest not in Peace

'He whispered me of a violated grave — of a disfigured body enshrouded, yet still breathing, still palpitating, still alive!'
From Poe's 'Berenice' (1835)

Poe was personally obsessed with being buried alive. Alcohol sent him into a trance, opium into a dream. He often did not know where he woke — or even in what body. During the slow illness of his wife Virginia from a broken blood vessel, she came back from the dead time and again, driving him mad. As he wrote just before his own dying: 'Her life was despaired of. I took leave of her forever and underwent all the agonies of her death. She recovered partially and again I hoped. At the end of a year the vessel broke again . . . Then again — again — again and even once again . . . I became insane, with long intervals of horrible sanity. During these fits of absolute unconsciousness, I drank, God only knows how often or how much.'

From these experiences came his obsessions with premature burial and the return of the dead. In the cinema, the first use of this theme seems to have been in Nordisk's *The Necklace of the Dead,* released by Bioscope in 1910. In this drama, a girl is nearly buried alive, wearing her engagement gift, a necklace. A thief comes to rob her tomb, attempts to grab the necklace and revives her. The next timely arrival is her fiancé, who saves her from the thief — altogether an ambiguous tale, where greed seems to be the secret of resurrection. Premature burial is also one of the minor obsessions of Carl Dreyer's masterpiece *Vampyr* of 1931, where the hero David Gray dreams of his own funeral.

The next film on the theme was a curious vehicle for Erich von Stroheim as an actor, *The Crime of Doctor Crespi* of 1935. In this, the *Hollywood Reporter* said that Stroheim 'out-Karloffs Karloff without a make-up', giving 'such a cruel, cold, malignant and malevolent portrayal of a fiend in human flesh, that one gets an insane urge to up and let him have it'. Perhaps Stroheim was revenging himself on the cinema for the ruin of his career as a director, but here he plays a role of a surgeon, who tyrannises the hospital which he dominates. When a rival doctor, who has married the girl that Stroheim loves, is injured in an automobile accident, Stroheim gives him a paralysing drug that makes him seem to be dead — and has him buried alive. Fortunately, he recovers from being a zombie, unlike the victim with another man's brain in another 'mad doctor' Stroheim vehicle, *The Lady and the Monster* of 1944, or the undead in Val Lewton's *I Walked with a Zombie* of 1943, which actually owed more to *Jane Eyre* and a series of newspaper articles on Haiti than to a rewrite of Edgar Allan Poe. In fact, the most chilling and Poe-like performance of a corpse brought back to life was Karloff's in Michael Curtiz's *The Walking Dead* of 1936. *(See Colour Section)*

Another Lewton-produced movie, however, did hark back to 'The Premature Burial', and that was Mark Robson's *The Isle of the Dead* of 1945, which also starred Karloff in a tale of weird doings on a Greek island. In the film, Katherine Emery played a middle-aged woman, capable of falling into cataleptic trances. Scared of being buried alive, she begged for tests to be made, if she did seem to die. They were all made and they all proved negative. She was buried — and in a famous scene, the camera

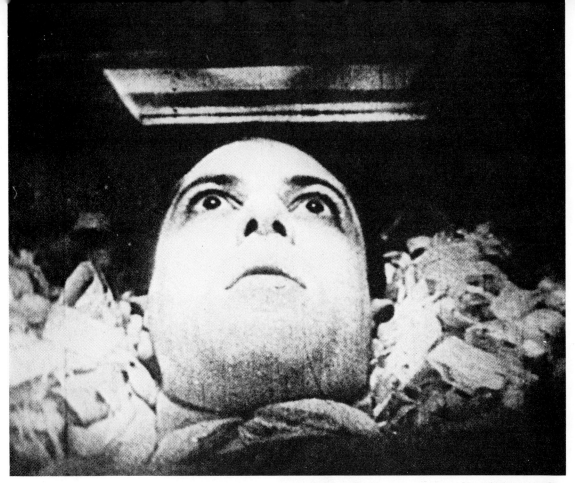

In Dreyer's *Vampyr* (1932), the hero dreams of being buried alive and looks up out of his own coffin.

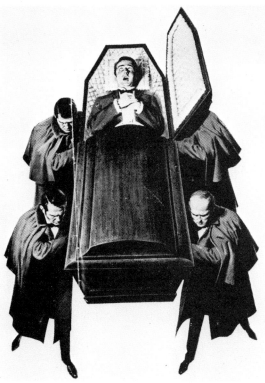

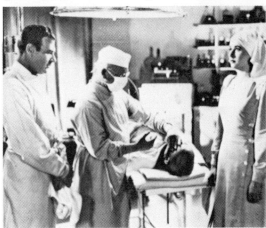

Stroheim enjoys the role of the mad doctor in *The Lady and the Monster* of 1944.

From the press-book of Roger Corman's version of *The Premature Burial* (1962).

The zombie appears to the maidens in *I Walked with a Zombie* (1943).

Katherin Emery wakes to see an angel of light and death in *The Isle of the Dead* (1945).

tracked in on her coffin as the music rose to a crescendo. There was a silence. Then the sound of water dripping. Then silence again. Then a muffled scream. Then the scratch, scratch, scratch of nails scratching at a coffin-lid. Fade out. All said, nothing shown. The true Lewton style, the nearest to the mood of Poe.

Yet where Lewton was the master of psychological horror through the imagination and the unseen, Roger Corman never used a scalpel where an axe would do. His version of *The Premature Burial,* made with Ray Milland in 1962, also included plot elements from Poe's 'Berenice'. In it, Ray Milland plays Guy Carrell, whose family suffers from catalepsy and who is mortally scared of being buried alive. He has even constructed a tomb for himself with enough methods of escape to satisfy a Houdini, including a final goblet of poison

Ray Milland is made mad in *The Premature Burial*.

Milland puts his wife into her grave.

if all should fail. He is persuaded to destroy this tomb and to marry, in order to cure his obsession. A kitten is found walled up in the house and a visit to the family crypt shows Guy that his father was, indeed, buried alive. The shock makes Guy collapse, as if dead – and he is buried as well because his wife's father wishes to use him for medical experiments. But when the grave-diggers come to resurrect him, he rises from the dead and kills them both. Proceeding on his path of revenge, he murders his medical father-in-law, then ties up his wife, throws her into the grave, and covers her up with earth. He is finally killed by a bullet from his sister's pistol although she knows that his dead wife is really at fault, for it is she who played on his fears of premature burial. *(See Colour Section)*

Corman's heavy-handed approach to

Then Milland himself ends finally dead in a burial no longer premature.

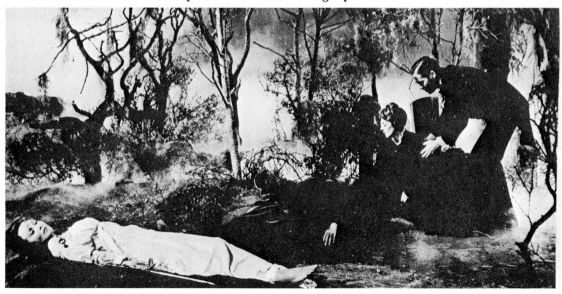

In *The Raven,* which united three of the great horror artists, Peter Lorre actually was metamorphosed from a raven into himself.

one stroke of genius which Corman contributed, was to use as his leading actors the ageing Karloff and Vincent Price, that master of the weary pregnant pause, and Peter Lorre, that prince of the perverse, until he died without resurrection after *The Raven.*

Yet never were there so many comings and goings back and forth from the grave as in Corman's version of *The Tomb of Ligeia.* In Poe's story, the dark-haired Ligeia refused to die, starting up from her death-bed with the terrible words: 'Man doth not yield him to the angels, *nor unto death utterly,* save only through the weakness of his feeble will.' She dies and is buried, and the hero marries again, the blonde Lady of Tremaine. Yet she also falls ill of some mysterious disease and dies. Her shrouded corpse seems to change shape, to become alive in front of his eyes. The shroud falls back and out stream 'huge masses of long and dishevelled hair; *it was blacker than the raven wings of the*

Poe was typical of a man, who had learned his technique in quickie films about space-monsters and other shockers. Although later a cult was to grow about the eight films which Corman perpetrated in the name of Poe, they had far more to do with the rising blood-and-thunder style of the new Hammer Gothic films of the late 1950s dealing with the Frankenstein and Dracula cults, than they had to do with the baroque subtleties of Edgar Allan Poe's ideas. The

Vincent Price stands by Ligeia's tomb, as her coffin is inserted.

He wears dark glasses, later stolen by a malevolent black cat and carried off up a crumbling tower as a harbinger of doom.

The fatal black cat attacks the blonde Lady of Tremaine

midnight! And now slowly opened *the eyes* of the figure which stood before me. "Here then, at least," I shrieked aloud, "can I never – can I never be mistaken – these are the full, and the black, and the wild eyes – of my lost love – of the lady – of the LADY LIGEIA".'

. . . and Vincent Price in Corman's *Ligeia*.

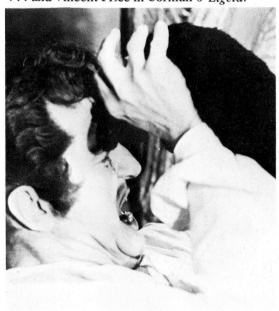

Price cannot believe that the Lady of Tremaine is turning back into the dead Ligeia.

In Poe's story, Ligeia comes back once from the tomb through the body of the Lady of Tremaine. In Corman's version, she rises again and again and again like a farcical Virginia with her broken blood vessels. As if in a black pantomine, Vincent Price has to kill the corpse time after time, as it comes back for more and more and more, even finally changing back to the Lady of Tremaine to provide a silly happy ending. Corman's Ligeia is like one of those aggression-objects bearing the director's face, which is put up in large Japanese stores for the employees to knock down, only to see it pop up again, always indestructible, always evilly grinning. While it is enjoyable knockabout, it loses Poe's sense of waiting for the evil to come. Corman had already used others of Poe's stories about the undead to make up his *Tales of Terror* of 1962 – 'Morella' and

Ligeia will not die – but finally involves Price in her blazing end.

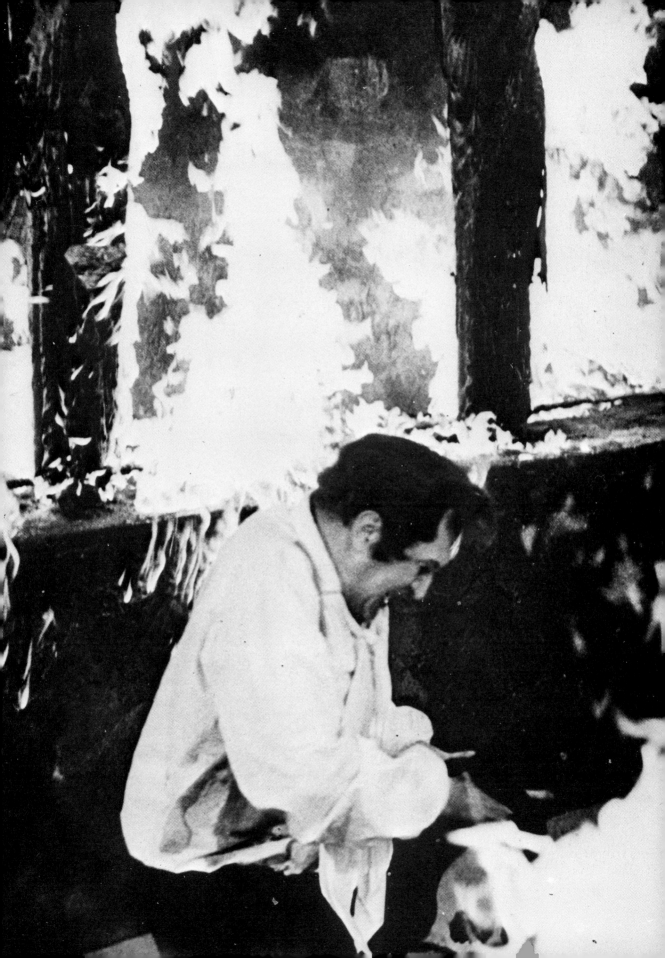

The poster of Corman's Ligeia . . . compared to Rackham's illustration of the story, which captures all Poe's sense of ominous waiting.

'The Facts of the Case of M. Valdemar''. This film was more successful than his *Ligeia* as it had Basil Rathbone starring with Vincent Price and Peter Lorre. In the first of the episodes, 'Morella', Vincent Price is consumed by flames as he grapples with his wife's mummy, now in the person of his dead daughter. In 'M. Valdemar', poor Price is kept alive by Rathbone playing the unscrupulous mesmerist Carmichael; when hypnosis gives up, Price disintegrates into corrupt ooze rather

The dead and the living change in 'Morella' in *Tales of Terror*.

Price decomposes over Rathbone when the hypnosis gives out in 'M. Valdemar'.

like burnt gravy, while hugging the mesmerist to death by fright. Lorre only appears in the third episode, which is a combination of 'The Black Cat' with 'The Cask of Amontillado', but he is superb as the drunken Montresor, walling up his wife alive with her lover Price. Unfortunately, he has walled up his own cat Pluto as well, and its howling gives him away to the police, who tear down the wall to find it perched on the heads of his

Price wonders whether the drunken Lorre suspects his liaison with Lorre's wife in 'The Cask of Amontillado'.

Pluto, the black cat, warns Lorre of his impending death, even though he carries out his revenge and walls up the lovers, despite Price's heart-rending last plea, 'For the love of God, Montresor.'

decomposed victims.

Corman is, in fact, better at treating Poe's material with humour rather than horror, particularly with Peter Lorre there to aid him. A crude Argentinian version of the same three tales, made by Enrique Carreras in 1960 and released in the United States under the title of *Master of Horror,* has more genuine terror in it than the Corman version, although the wife is drowned in the Cask of Amontillado rather like a Duchess of Clarence. Even the two Italian horror films of 1963 which tried to jump on the Poe hearse as it was rolling through the box-offices – Antonio Margheriti's *La Danza Macabra* and Alberto Martino's *Horror* – adapt 'Berenice' and 'The Premature Burial' in an *outré* way that is rather disturbing, especially when that

A publicity still for *Tales of Terror* shows Corman's sense of humour.

Rackham also illustrated the walling-up of Fortunato in 'The Cask of Amontillado'.

Barbara Steele eyes her victim in *La Danza Macabra* of 1963.

Lugosi contemplates his travelling earth-boxes in his famous *Dracula* (1932).

The undead advance during their ball in *The Fearless Vampire-killers* (1967).

queen of the Italian chillers, Barbara Steele, is on the screen, playing at Berenice.

Others have dug in the Poe cemetery that Corman resurrected so thoroughly. There was Gordon Hessler's *The Oblong Box* of 1968 and Alexandre Astruc's *The Oval Portrait* of 1969. In both of these films, the dead become alive, and the living slip into death as if they have always been disembodied. But neither of these films about the undead, directly influenced by Poe's stories, was as effective in recreating his unearthly mood as those films indirectly influenced by Poe through other writers – particularly Bram Stoker, whose novel 'Dracula' had set Shreck's Nosferatu and

the later Lugosi voyaging with their coffins, and whose tradition of the undead created such camp masterpieces as Polanski's *The Fearless Vampire-killers* and underground classics such as *Night of the Living Dead*.

For Poe, too, was undead. His influence worked directly through the words he left behind him, and indirectly through the mood of unease, which penetrated all the other writers and artists and film-makers who had read him. His next great theme was one which he had inherited from Ancient Egypt, the theme of the Black Cat, signifying the God of Death. To Poe, it meant revenge as well as death; but its myth still haunts us all.

Omen of Death

'An incarnate Night-Mare that I had no power to shake off — incumbent eternally upon my heart*!'*
From Poe's 'The Black Cat' (1843)

'Poe, you are avenged!'
Lugosi in The Raven (1935)

Although black cats are considered lucky in modern English and French folk-lore, they were considered the familiars of witches, also one of the shapes of the Devil in medieval Europe. As such, the cat appears in Christiansen's early classic on witchcraft, *Haxan*. A recent film of Bulgakov's *The Master and Margarita* sticks to the original novel in showing the Devil as a great black cat. Edgar Allan Poe in his own story 'The Black Cat' consciously used the legend of evil. The cat of the eventual wife-murderer was called Pluto by him and 'was a remarkably large and beautiful

This charming cat-woman French postcard of 1900 shows the black cat as a symbol of good luck.

animal, entirely black, and sagacious to an astonishing degree. In speaking of his intelligence, my wife, who at heart was not a little tinctured with superstition, made frequent allusion to the ancient popular notion, which regarded all black cats as witches in disguise. Not that she was ever *serious* upon this point . . .'

Perhaps she should have been. In Poe's story, the husband is possessed by the spirit of the perverse and by drink. First he loves his Pluto cat, then he cuts out one of its eyes, then he hangs it. His house immediately burns down, leaving the burned image of a gigantic hanging cat on the plaster of one wall. So he picks up another black one-eyed cat with a white patch of fur on its chest which grows into the shape of the gallows. Trying to kill it, he hits his wife over the head with an axe and kills her. To hide the body, he walls up the corpse in his cellar, as in *The Cask of Amontillado*. Unfortunately, he has walled up the omen of evil as well, and as the police come to investigate the cellar, they hear from the bricked-in tomb, 'one long, loud, and continuous scream, utterly anomalous and inhuman — a howl — a wailing shriek, half of horror and half of triumph, such as might have arisen only out of hell, conjointly from the throats of the damned in their agony and of the demons that exult in the damnation'. It is the black cat speaking from the tomb and consigning its master to the rope he had used on it.

In films, Poe's black cat was not used as a major symbol of evil until two German films of 1926 and 1933. The second, *Five Extraordinary Tales*, was a remake by Michael Oswald of his own film of seven years

Beardsley shows his haunting black cat sitting on the victim's head.

The black cat stalks the passages of the gothic castle in *The Black Cat* in 1934.

five tales – one of the first compendia of horror stories put on the screen and imitated from Leni's *Waxworks* of 1924. Two of the five tales were said to be taken from Poe, 'The Black Cat' and 'The System of Dr. Tarr and Professor Fether'. Yet the derivation is more in mood than plot, because Poe himself does not personify Death or the Devil in these stories. Oswald's world was more Germanic and Gothic and Faustian than Poe's world of the macabre.

In fact, Poe's name seems to have been dragged in only to set a mood, as it was into the extraordinary Lugosi and Karloff film of 1934, directed by Edgar G. Ulmer, which owed far more to the career of the black magician Aleister Crowley than to Poe's plot. To one critic, however, its claustrophobic and unhealthy atmosphere does evoke 'a definite feeling of Poe – allied perhaps with a Kafkaesque sense of entrapment, futility and hopelessness. *(See Colour Section)*

before; it was released in the United States under the title of *The Living Dead*. Conrad Veidt, who had played the sleep-walking killer in *Dr. Caligari*, played Death in the first version, while Paul Wegener, who had played the *Student of Prague* and the *Golem*, played Death in the second version of the

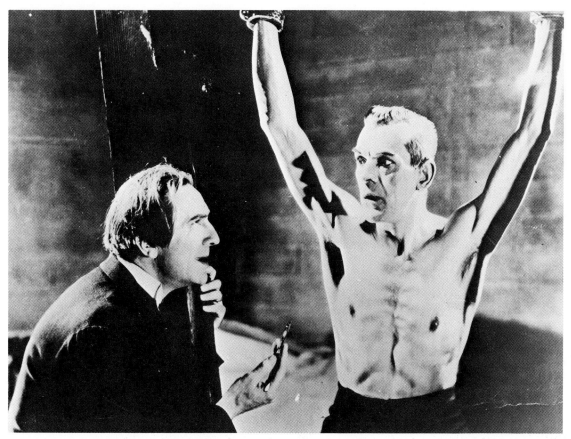

Lugosi begins to flay his enemy Karloff alive with the words: 'Did you ever see an animal skinned? That's what I'm going to do – tear the skin from your body – slowly – bit by bit!' He is shot, but as he dies, he blows up the whole castle.

The black cat does actually appear as a device to frighten the heroine, carried by the black hooded figure of Karloff, the head of a Hungarian cult of devil-worshippers; but in the film, the devil-beast looks like a limp sort of household pussy. The real Big Cats are the black-dressed Lugosi and Karloff himself in their most chilling confrontation which ends with Lugosi beginning to flay Karloff alive as a prelude to blowing up his whole castle (an echo of 'The Fall of the House of Usher'). One incident and speech relate this exercise in mannered terror to Poe's story. Karloff has introduced the black cat to terrify Lugosi, who throws a knife at it and kills it. Karloff then dwells on Lugosi's extreme phobia for cats, 'an all-consuming horror – of cats'. But Karloff has cast himself in the role of Lugosi's tormentor, even preserving the body of Lugosi's first wife in a glass case in his chart-room.

When Lugosi first sees the pickled body of his dead wife, Karloff suavely says: 'I have cared for her tenderly and well.'

Ulmer's direction of the film and his inventive and brooding use of atmospherics and contrasted black-and-white effects are

The brooding lighting of *The Black Cat* is like the best of Beardsley.

possibly more faithful to the world of Poe than those of any other film-maker; he is, indeed, the Aubrey Beardsley of the cinema as an illustrator of Poe. Even though the whole feeling of the piece was Central European and derived more from the recent success of Tod Browning's *Dracula* with Lugosi and James Whale's *Frankenstein* with Karloff, yet Ulmer's sense of atmosphere and the bizarre twists of his plot showed him more in key with Poe's disordered and contrived stories than many more faithful imitators were to be.

The film was successful enough for Universal to push Lugosi and Karloff the next year into another macabre chiller called *The Raven,* which was even more tenuously linked to Poe. In fact, other than the perennial black bird of ill-omen, now stuffed and perched on Lugosi's desk, and a pendulum-plus-shrinking-room hidden

Ulmer's version of *The Black Cat* does include a black mass, relating the symbol to the Devil.

in Lugosi's private torture chamber, the chief link with Poe seemed to be a dance to 'The Spirit of Poe' by the Judge's daughter, played by Irene Ware. The director, Louis Friedlander (later called Lew Landers), had little talent beyond reproducing a run-of-the-mill 'mad doctor' feature, with Lugosi playing a surgeon more in love with unspeakable experiments than spoken Edgar, and Karloff playing a gangster disfigured by Lugosi, who seems to like keeping Karloff's nerve-ends raw while anaesthetising the audience with a soporific performance.

Karloff, indeed, lurches slack-jawed through his part, as if he was acting in some nightmare, until he finally turns the tables on Lugosi. The dialogue is on the level of statements such as, 'Maybe if a man is ugly, he does ugly things,' followed by the answer, 'You are saying something profound'.

In fact, crass imitations of 'The Spirit of Poe' served him worse than those great writers who were influenced by him or those great film-makers who were true to his influence. Four American films of the

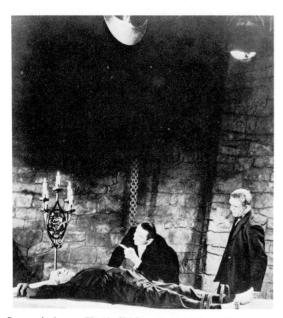

Lugosi shows Karloff his private Pit and Pendulum in *The Raven* (1935).

Karloff begins as a gangster . . . then is disfigured by Lugosi and falls into his power.

Lugosi horrifies his guests, when he introduces them to Karloff, his new butler.

Karloff has had enough of Lugosi . . .

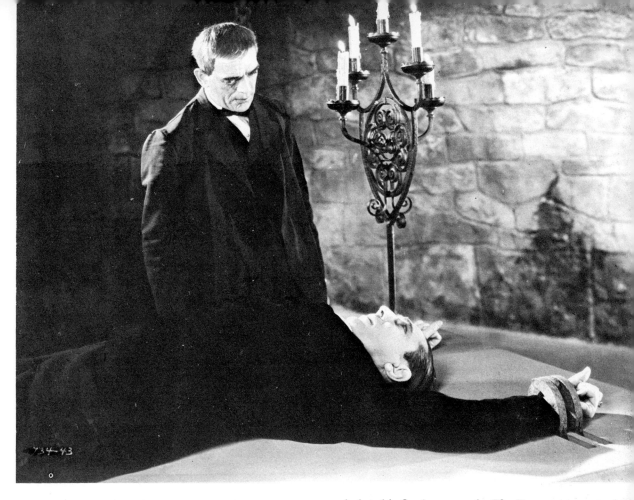

. . . and plots his final revenge in *The Raven*.

Pig-Men...Wolf-Women...
Thoughtful Human Apes
—And His Masterpiece...
The Panther Woman . . .
Throbbing to the Hot
Flush of New Found Love!

ISLAND OF LOST SOULS

A Paramount Picture

WITH

H. G. Wells' Surging
Rhapsody of Romance,
Adventure and Terror!

Re-released by Universal Pictures

period were particularly gripping on the theme of the cat as evil or devil. The first was the film of H. G Wells's 'The Island of Dr. Moreau' retitled *The Island of Lost Souls*. It made a great play of the Panther Woman, who incites the half-beasts, half-men to kill their mad surgeon Charles Laughton. Lugosi actually played in this film as well, but his wooden features were luckily hidden behind a mass of hair as the wolf-man (rather reminiscent of many actors who have played the orang-outang in the films of 'The Murder in the Rue Morgue').

The other three Poe-derived films were in Val Lewton's nine thrillers in the early 1940s; they were *Cat People, The Leopard Man* and *The Curse of the Cat People*. In the first Simone Simon plays the Eastern European woman who seems to turn into a black panther to kill her rival. Lewton was forced in one shot to show the panther outside its cage in the zoo rather than to suggest it; but the great sequence of the

The cat is only a household menace in *The Curse of the Cat People* (1944).

The poster of the film exploited the ambiguity between black panther and woman.

Simone Simon plays the cat-haunted witch-woman in *Cat People* (1942). She tells her lover: 'I am a refugee – a refugee from the past – from evil things you could never know or understand.'

film remains the one in which the rival girl's clothes are ripped to shreds, while she swims in a pool and hears all around her the terror of the invisible Black Cat. *The Leopard Man* was less successful, its plot relating to an escaped leopard which kills one woman, while a killer pretends to be the leopard and murders two more women. The final feline film, *The Curse of the Cat People* still had Simone Simon as the ghost of the Black Panther Woman, but a weak script changed her from black to white witch, her malevolence all turned to being a good fairy to her rival's child. As a legend of good and evil, it was to be outclassed by Cocteau's *La Belle at la Bête,* also made in 1944, where the beauty changed the malevolent cat-beast man into a fairy prince.

The Lewton films were far truer to the spirit of Poe than the farcical Universal remake of *The Black Cat* with Lugosi in 1941. Lugosi was already sinking into his decline with the descent of horror pictures into cheap B-Films and comedy-terror vehicles. Although the cast of the picture was distinguished, including Basil Rathbone, Broderick Crawford, Alan Ladd, Gale Sondergaard and Gladys Cooper, the contrived script and ordinary direction had little to do either with Poe or entertainment.

The Beast menaces the Beauty in *La Belle et la Bète* **(1944).**

Again *The Black Cat* of 1941 is all household pussy . . . and not very menacing.

The plot revolves round a crazed woman who loves cats and leaves all her money to them after she is murdered by her relatives. The dialogue in the gloomy house is at the level of 'everything around here is for the cats, that's why the place is going to the dogs'. The failure of the film, allied with the failure of *The Cat Creeps* of 1946 in which a murdered woman's spirit lives on in her cat's body, put an end to Hollywood's

interest in the subject for nearly twenty years, until Corman appeared to revive Poe's harbingers of death with the best of his comic-horror films, *The Raven* of 1963.

In this gothic romp on themes from Poe, Karloff and Vincent Price and Peter Lorre were united in their ghoulish enjoyment. A quarter of a century before, Karloff had drowned Price in a butt of malmsey wine in *Tower of London*. This time he joined Price and Lorre in an unholy trio of tired 15th century sorcerers, not exactly competent at their trade. Although Price is distinguished with his skeletons and alchemies, and although Karloff looks grave and shows his seventy-five years as Dr. Scarabus, it is Lorre's triumphant raven-song. Karloff has actually changed Lorre into the black bird of prey itself on the bust of Pallas – although later released from his tar and feathers, Lorre still manages to look like a carrion fowl. He is as silly and gleeful as a schoolboy with his sorceries. In Price's

The actors look as if they cannot believe the film in which they are appearing in *The Cat Creeps* (1946).

american-international
presents
EDGAR ALLAN POE'
THE Raven
in
PANAVISION & PATHÉCOLOR
STARRING
Vincent PRICE
Peter LORRE
Boris KARLOFF

The black bird is metamorphosed into Lorre
himself . . . who is not good at casting spells

Price is not much better at casting spells himself

family crypt, where they have gone to steal some hair from Price's dead father, Lorre observes, 'Gee! Hard place to keep clean, huh?' just before the father resurrects himself. With a comic climax of mad cannons and snakes as neckties, it is Corman's best travesty of Poe, and in a class with his other gothic parody, *Comedy of Terrors*.

Although *The Raven* has been treated as a subject for many short and animated films, and although the idea of a murderer pretending to be a 'Cat' was used most successfully in the early thriller, *The Cat and the Canary,* Poe's theme of the black beast as the warning of death has only been used spectacularly and well once in recent films. It is worth ignoring a remake of Poe's theme in 1965, entitled *The Black Cat* and directed by Harold Hoffman, in which the lead man thinks the beast is a reincarnation

The three sorcerers are not good at their trade in *The Raven* . . . and Price gets hoisted on his own chandelier.

Karloff gets ready to torture the two rival sorcerers in *The Raven* . . . but all ends in blazing ruin as usual.

The claw of 'The Cat' menaces Laura la Plante in *The Cat and the Canary* of 1927.

The black cat at least howls and has one eye in the 1965 remake.

of his dead father and walls it up accidentally – also *Eye of the Cat* of 1969, where ravening household pussies pursue Gayle Hunnicut up a ladder. The only successful use of the theme was in the Yugoslav picture *The Switchboard Operator,* where the black cat lies on the body of the girl, waiting for her lover, but soon to be a naked drowned corpse on a mortuary slab. It was as ominous as that brute who had made Poe's wife-murderer wretched, starting him 'from dreams of unutterable fear, to find the hot breath of *the thing* upon my face, and its vast weight – an incarnate Night-Mare that I had no power to shake off – incumbent eternally upon my *heart!*'

The black cat is the symbol of death to *The Switchboard Operator* (1967).

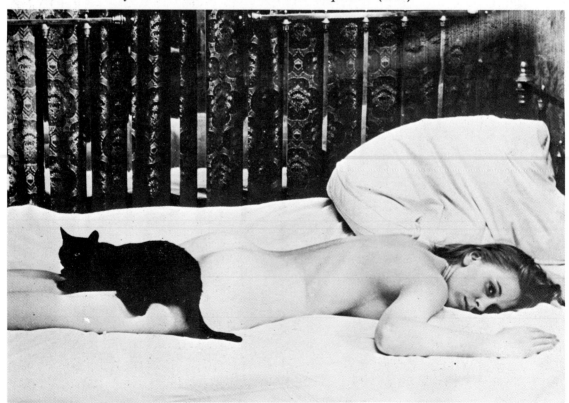

The black cat leaps in revenge at the second wife in Corman's *Ligeia*.

The Beat and the Blade

' "Death", I said, "any death but that of the pit!" Fool! might I have not known that into the pit it was the object of the burning iron to urge me?'
From Poe's 'The Pit and the Pendulum' (1843) (See cover from an illustration by Arthur Rackham.)

Traditionally, the heart is the symbol for love – either love present, love pining, or the torments of love. But the heart is also the pump of the blood. One repetitive and haunting quatrain reveals the obsessions of Poe, fearing the thudding beat of the blood, the ticking of time, the laboured gasps of the ill:

I thought I heard a distant tick,
It said, 'I am so sick, so sick!
O Death, come quick, come quick, come quick,
Come quick, come quick, come quick, COME
    QUICK!'

In his story, 'The Tell-Tale Heart', Poe turns his psychological problems into a short masterpiece of avenging conscience.

Three early postcards show the heart bringing joy to the trenches . . . the heart fading and falling like an apple from the tree . . . and the heart burning lovers like moths in its flame.

Heureuse Année !

The murderer kills his benefactor, an old man, because the old man obsesses him with a blue, blind and filmy vulture's eye. He dismembers the old man and puts him under the floorboards. Perversity and vanity make him take the police into the room where the pieces of the body lie hidden. Then, he hears what he thinks is the steady beating of the dead man's heart.

'The noise arose over all and continually increased. It grew louder – louder – *louder!* And still the men chatted pleasantly, and

The pressbook of the 1960 version of *The Tell-tale Heart* emphasised its beat.

smiled. Was it possible they heard not? Almighty God! – no, no! They heard! – they suspected! – They *knew*! – they were making a mockery of my horror! – this I thought, and this I think. But anything was better than this agony! Anything was more tolerable than this derision! I could bear those hypocritical smiles no longer! I felt that I must scream or die! And now – again! – hark! louder! louder! louder! *louder!*

"'Villains''', I shrieked, "dissemble no

Rackham's murderer hears the beating of the heart!

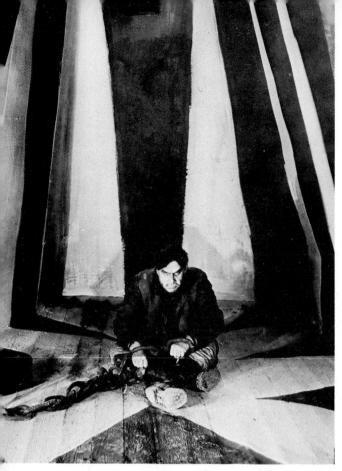

The madman in *Dr. Caligari* recollects his crime under sets that influenced the 1927 American production of *The Tell-tale Heart*.

more! I admit the deed! – tear up the planks! here, here! – it is the beating of his hideous heart!" '

So Poe's story inspired D. W. Griffith to his chilling *silent* sequence of the culmination of repetitive action in *The Avenging Conscience* of 1914. The theme of 'The Tell-Tale Heart' was to be used another ten times in the cinema in silent and sound films, relying on Griffith's interpretation and the montage effect of Poe, whose hyphens and exclamation marks provide

Rackham's endpiece to Poe's story shows the gothic horror of the tale.

the nearest thing to a cut horror sequence in literature. In 1927, Charles F. Klein directed an experimental and expressionist version of the Poe story, trying and failing to make an American Dr. Caligari, with doors opening at wild angles on the guilty madman, trapped in the sets. In 1934, a British production of the story, directed by Brian Desmond-Hurst, was faithful to the original, although it ended up with the title, *Bucket of Blood*. Particularly good were the sequences where the young murderer is driven mad by the old man's blind and veiled eye. The film actually begins and ends (as in Dr. Caligari) in an asylum where the young man recollects his crime.

Jules Dassin made the fourth version of *The Tell-Tale Heart* for MGM in 1941, starring Joseph Schildkraut in a short film that won the Oscar of that year. Dassin made the young murderer retarded and feeble-minded, to explain his obsession about the old man's eye. He had sound effects to complete the Griffith techniques, mixing the dripping of a tap and the ticking of a clock into the thudding of the heartbeat. He also made Schildkraut play myths in mime, as if still in the days of the silent film. The words do not intrude on the hallucinatory sounds that torment the murderer into confession. As Schildkraut wrote in his memoirs, 'the film was to a great extent in pantomime, accompanied by movie and sound effects. In fact I did not speak more than four sentences in the whole picture.'

In a French horror mixture concocted by Jean Faurez in 1950, *Histoires Extraordinaires,* Fernand Ledoux and Jules Berry played 'The Tell-Tale Heart' with 'The Cask of Amontillado' and two tales by Thomas de Quincey. The film really owed more to Grand Guignol than to the macabre imagination of Poe, and was chiefly interesting in linking two of the three Poe tales that deal with the concealment of a body under a floor or behind a wall (as Corman was later to do in his *Tales of Terror,* using 'The Cask of Amontillado' and 'The Black Cat' in his episode with Peter Lorre). The next feature using the theme was, indeed, even

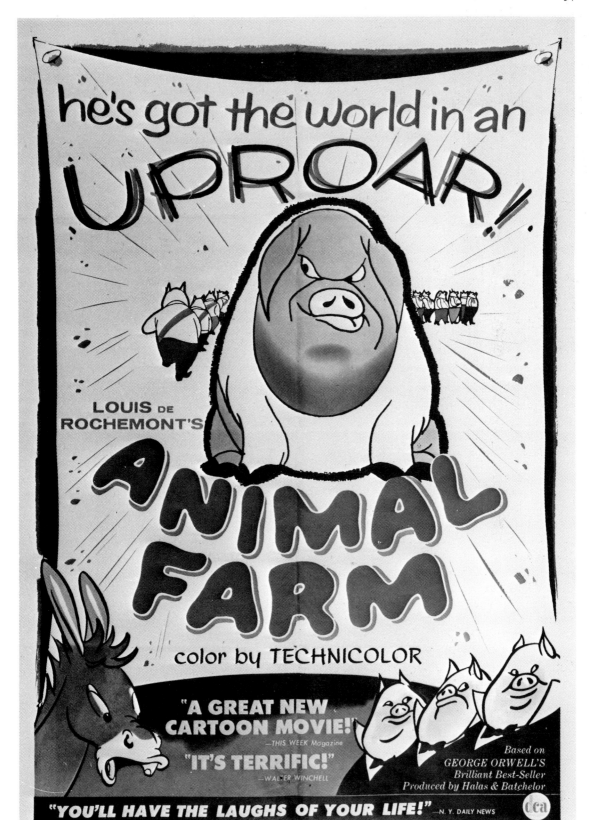

The old man with his blind eye starts up in horror.

worse – W. Lee Wilder's *Manfish* of 1956, starring Lon Chaney Jr. in an improbable modernised hash of 'The Gold-Bug' with 'The Tell-Tale Heart'. The imaginary thudding of the betraying heart was translated into the actual bursting of bubbles from an oxygen cylinder attached to a drowned corpse. Out of genius and derangement, crass science!

The theme was far better treated in a series of television and short animated films. William Cameron Menzies did it under the title of *Heartbeat* for the box in 1950, again using a pantomime technique for the murderer borrowed from Griffith and Dassin, but using Poe's words heavily in a voice-over on the soundtrack. Stanley Baker narrated and acted a British short version in 1953 in a virtuoso

Laurence Payne uses his weapon in the 1960 version of *The Tell-tale Heart*.

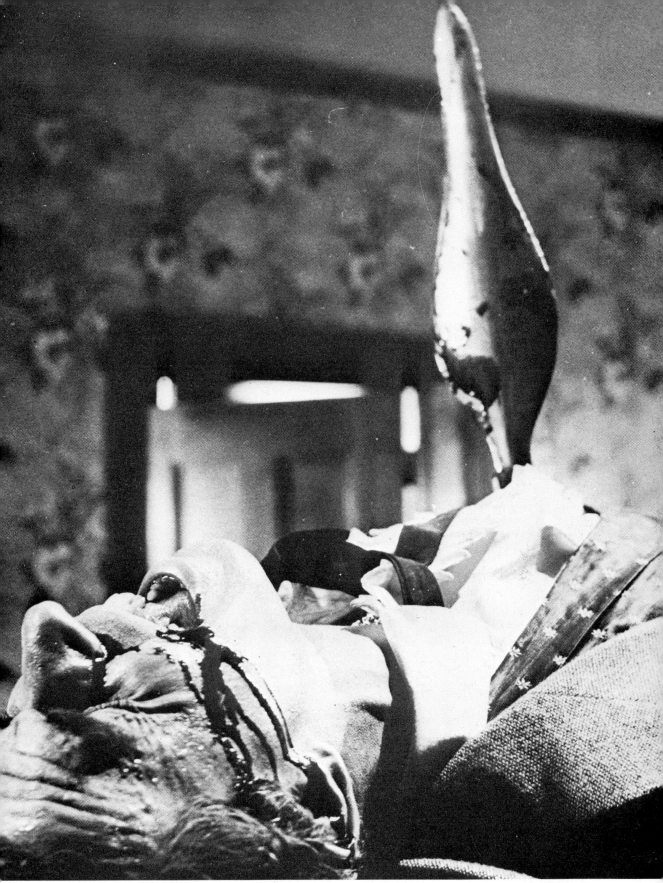

Above and over page: **Blood and violence characterised the British version of 'The Tell-tale Heart.'**

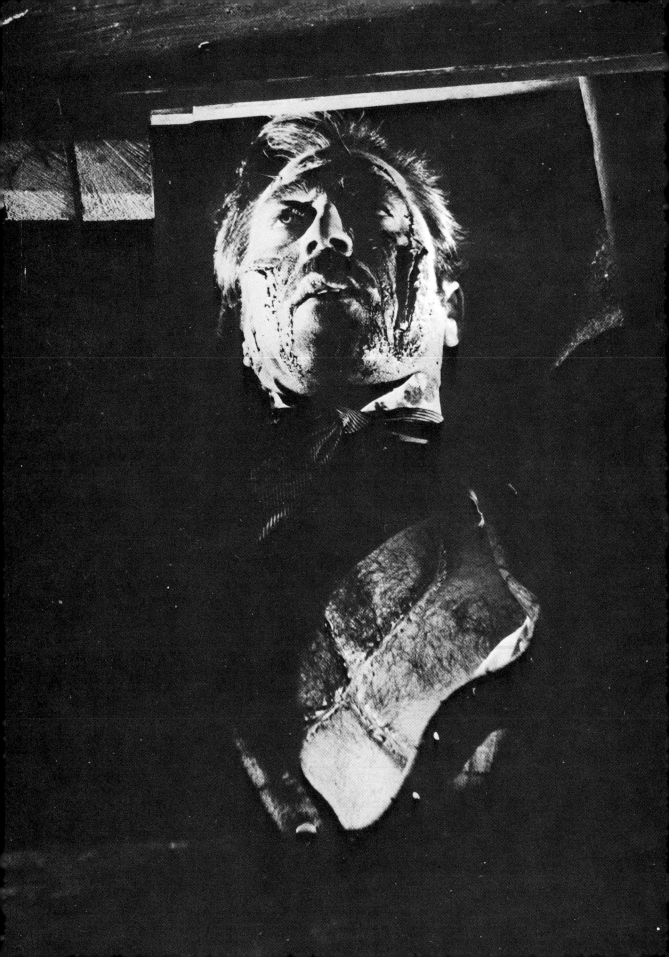

theatrical performance. That same year, a lurid cartoon version appeared from UPA, produced by Paul Julian and Ted Parmelee, and narrated by James Mason. It was quite successful and proved to be the precursor for a most successful cartoon version of George Orwell's fable *Animal Farm* two years later, itself an essay in totalitarian terror with pigs playing the evil role of Poe's cats.

One more full-length British feature called *The Tell-Tale Heart* has been remade in 1960. It was directed by Ernest Morris for the Danzigers and it starred Laurence Payne as Edgar Allan Poe, dreaming that he was the young murderer of the story as Walthall did in the earlier versions of *The Avenging Conscience* and *The Raven,* and waking from his nightmare to find that the dream events had really begun. The film was bloodier than the original and the material prolonged by the voyeuristic obsessions of Payne for Adrienne Corri, and by his need to resurrect the body from under the floor-boards, in order to cut out the tell-tale heart and bury it in the garden, from where it mysteriously returned to its place under the floor. The best thing in the film was the hidden eroticism of Miss Corri, who was finally to show her full range in the rape sequence with the *droogs* in *The Clockwork Orange.*

Below: **Adrienne Corri is assaulted by the *droogs* in *The Clockwork Orange.***

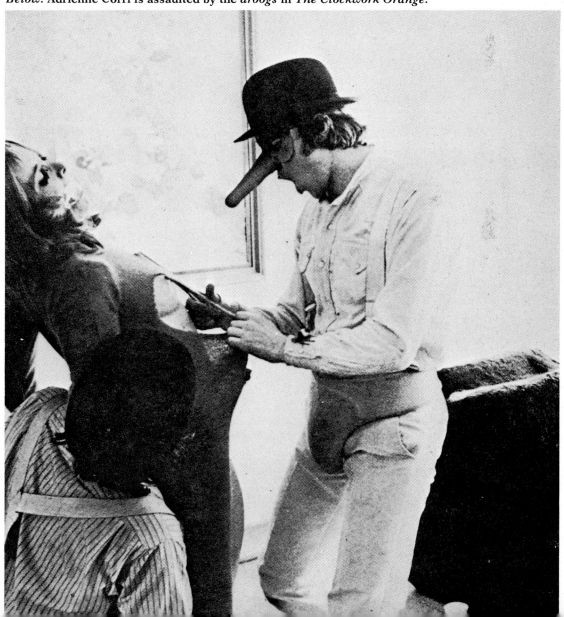

Rackham again captures the full horror of the Pit and the Pendulum.

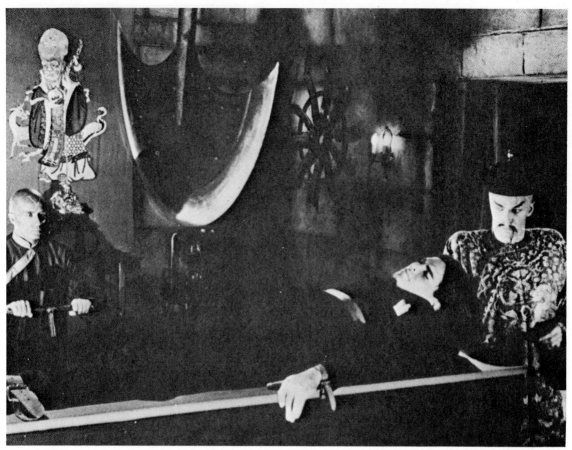

Henry Brandon as Fu Manchu tortures his western victim in his secret tomb that can dominate the world.

Poe's obsession with the slow relentless beat of death and the hours was shown in his most famous torture story, 'The Pit and the Pendulum'. In this, the Inquisition puts the prisoner in a rat-infested dungeon with walls that become red-hot and shrink and force him towards a horrible death in the hellish pit in the middle of the room. *(See Cover)* Before using this torture, the Inquisition binds him on to a rack, while from a figure of Time on the ceiling, a giant scythe-sharp pendulum slowly swings down, dropping towards his chest. Poe's writing shows his horror of a slow waiting death such as his child-wife Virginia suffered from her breaking blood-vessels.

'What boots it to tell of the long, long hours of horror more than mortal, during which I counted the rushing vibrations of the steel! Inch by inch – line by line – with a descent only appreciable at intervals that seemed ages – down and still down it came! Days passed – it might have been that many days passed – ere it swept so closely over me as to fan me with its acrid breath. The odour of the sharp steel forced itself into my nostrils. I prayed – I wearied heaven with my prayer for its more speedy descent. I grew frantically mad, and struggled to force myself upward against the sweep of the fearful scimitar. And then I fell suddenly calm, and lay smiling at the glittering death, as a child at some rare bauble.'

It was too good a cinematic scene to miss. Henri Desfontaines first did it in 1909 in a faithful version released by Bioscope, which only departed from Poe's plot by having the Inquisitor finally hurl himself into the Pit. Alice Guy-Blanche then used it in a Solax short feature in 1913, starring Darwin Kerr and Blanche Cornwall. It was also faithful to Poe's story within the conventions of the time – as the advertisements said, the

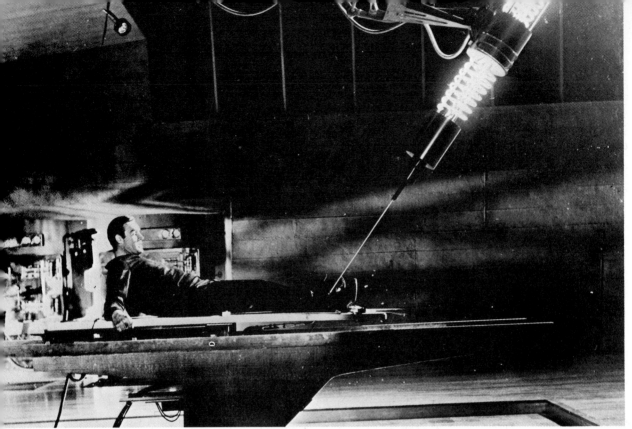

James Bond waits for an unpleasant death in *Goldfinger* (1964).

scenes mirrored 'Poe's compellingly grue-some, but not repellent, verbal rhapsody'. The hero, as in the original story, was saved on the brink of the pit by the arrival of French troops in Toledo.

Two other appearances of the actual torture mechanisms were in films that had precious little to do with Poe's story – *The Raven* of 1935 and *The Drums of Fu Manchu* of 1940. Presumably the Oriental villain had gone to the West for a native technique to terrify his prisoner, as Spectre

was to do in a more modernised form to James Bond, substituting a slow castrating laser beam for the old-fashioned pendulum.

In his Poe revival, Corman was twice to make *The Pit and the Pendulum*, once for real in 1961, and once for farce in a three-day romp in 1965 under the title of *Dr. G. and the Bikini Machine*. In the first version there is a hidden torture chamber in a Spanish castle on the sea; there Vincent Price, playing the Castilian aristocrat, has seen his father bury his

Dr. G.'s robot girls look more like a line-up from Busby Berkeley as they move about their murderous tasks.

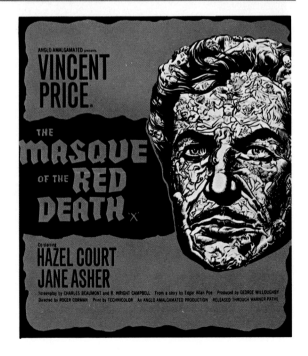

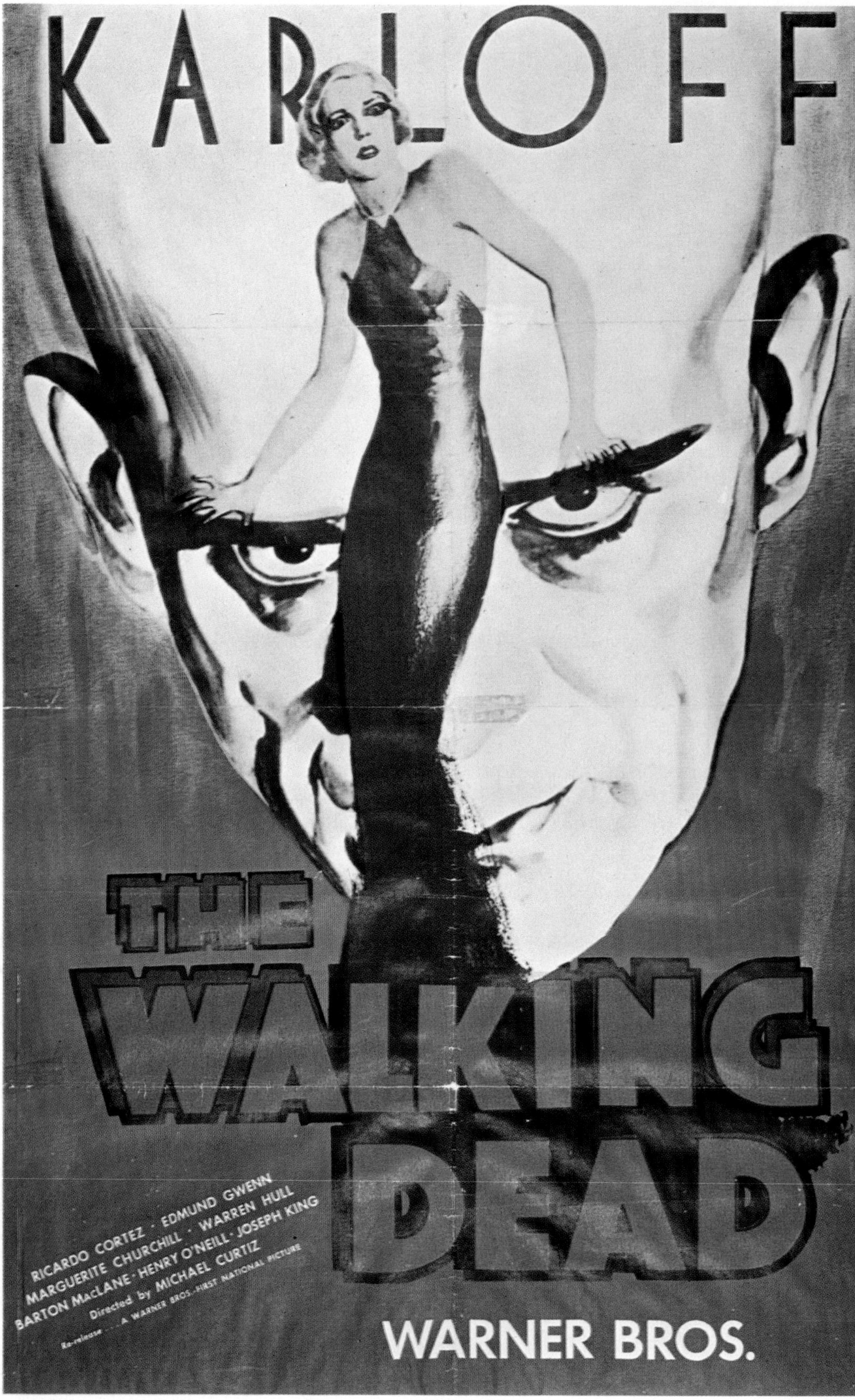

KARLOFF

THE WALKING DEAD

RICARDO CORTEZ · EDMUND GWENN
MARGUERITE CHURCHILL · WARREN HULL
BARTON MacLANE · HENRY O'NEILL · JOSEPH KING
Directed by MICHAEL CURTIZ
Re-release ·· A WARNER BROS.–FIRST NATIONAL PICTURE

WARNER BROS.

Yet Dr G.'s sharp pendulum is the authentic Poe item.

mother alive and murder her lover. His wife, played by Barbara Steele, plots to drive him insane, but he pops her into an Iron Maiden and straps her brother under the pendulum before finally plunging himself into the pit. *(See Colour Section)* There is a little of Poe in the film and even Corman seems weary of the same old style. Only Price does something for it with one good creepy line in the torture chamber, *'This room was my father's life!'*

Dr. G. and the Bikini Machine is much more fun and much further from Poe. Although the first half is a routine AIP thriller with Frankie Avalon, the second half in the torture chamber becomes a mad panto-mime farce, with Vincent Price behaving like a cross between Dr. Caligari and Mack Sennett, with his robot maidens in gold bikinis and his occasional victims darting between rack and spiked wheel and Iron Maiden.

Two more major versions of *The Pit and the Pendulum* were made, the first by the talented French director Alexandre Astruc in 1963. In some critic's opinion, this is one of the best Poe films ever made. The other use of the material was in Harald Reinl's interesting *Die Schlangengrube und Das Pendel* (also called *The Blood Demon*) of 1967. This film starred Christopher Lee as Count Regula, a resurrected vampire, who throws clean-cut Lex Barker into the castle pit to be cut up by a descending pendulum. A crucifix helps Barker escape and the castle crumbles to dust. The film really has more to do with *Dracula* than with Poe, but the castle is diabolical enough for a Bosch infernal vision or a Poe nightmare. And briefly it does capture the terror of the remorseless beat of inevitable death, the pendulum as terminal metronome, the 'inch by inch — line by line' slow wasting of Edgar Allan Poe.

Cobwebbed crypts are a staple of the cinema from *Dracula* to *The Blood Demon*.

The Conqueror Worm

'And Darkness and Decay and the Red Death held illimitable dominion over all.'
From Poe's 'The Masque of the Red Death' (1842)
'The House is the Monster.'
Roger Corman on The Fall of the House of Usher (1960)

Poe had a vision of human society, which he saw as a crowd chasing a Phantom evermore through a theatre.

   . . . But see, amid the mimic rout
     A crawling shape intrude!
     A blood-red thing that writhes from out
     The scenic solitude!
     It writhes! – it writhes! – with mortal pan
     The mimes become its food,
     And the angels sob at vermin fangs
     In human gore imbued.

     Out – out are the lights – out all!
     And, over each quivering form,
     The curtain, a funeral pall,
     Comes down with the rush of a storm,
     And the angels, all pallid and wan,
     Uprising, unveiling, affirm
     That the play is the tragedy, 'Man',
     And its hero the Conqueror Worm.

Roger Corman, in one of his more baroque moods and in order to get Poe's name on the billboards outside the cinemas to bring in the audience, filmed Price declaiming the poem of 'The Conqueror Worm' and tacked it on to the end of an English horror film, made in 1968 and called The Witchfinder General; it cast Price as Matthew Hopkins, the 17th century scourge of the witches, and had nothing to do with Poe at all. The film was gory and well-made by Michael Reeves, who died soon afterwards, proving in some way that the Conqueror Worm still triumphed.

Yet Price in his best role for Corman, Prince Prospero, the disciple of Satan in The Masque of the Red Death, played to the full the intention of Poe in his poem and

'. . . With its Phantom chased for evermore
By a crowd that seize it not . . .'
W. Heath Robinson's illustration to Poe's poem.

in his story derived from it. The great Lon Chaney had first used Poe's 'Red Death' in his entrance into the masked ball in The Phantom of the Opera, made as far back as 1925. While Poe's Red Death represented the Plague itself, which was to kill all the reckless revellers in Prince Prospero's castle, Chaney's skull mask hid the even more horrible face of Chaney himself, playing the Phantom of the Opera, flitting

Lon Chaney enters the Opera Ball as the Red Death.

about like the Phantom never seized by Poe's manic crowd. Although the film was silent and shot in black and white, Chaney's entrance as the Red Death was sometimes tinted crimson to add to its menace.

The great success of *The Phantom of the Opera* really led to the first upsurge of the horror movie, particularly when Chaney played the lead. Although he did not play any other Poe-inspired films, 'The Masque of the Red Death' was to be the peak of the career of Vincent Price, who was to be the leading star of the second upsurge of horror films in the 1960s. Corman's version of 1964 added to Poe's story another medieval tale by him, 'Hop-Frog', in which a dwarf jester has his revenge on a bully king and his Councillors by dragging them up to the ceiling and burning them alive, while they are disguised as apes. Henri Desfontaines had made a version of *Hop-Frog* as far back as 1910; but its amalgamation by Corman with *The Masque of the Red Death* filled out Poe's story to make a most satisfactory film. In fact, although Corman's movie lacks the

He reveals his own more terrifying face.

intellectual rigors of Bergman's *The Seventh Seal,* its use of the figure of Death and its ending, where Death's messengers report to their Master that only the dwarf jester and five others remain alive in all the world, has a quality worthy of Poe and Bergman's own vision of the plague and the apocalypse.

The colour of the film is one of its main distinctions. *(See Colour Section)* The scenes, which were brilliantly shot by the later

Rackham's drawing of Hop-Frog's terrible revenge.

Corman's version of Hop-Frog's revenge in *The Masque of the Red Death*.

One of Death's messengers reports to her master in Corman's *The Masque of the Red Death* . . .

And Death is again personified in Bergman's *The Seventh Seal*.

Jane Asher is scared . . . and given a bath by Price as Prince Prospero to make her fit for his satanic revels.

Price humiliates his guests in *The Masque of the Red Death*.

The Red Death enters — and Price is the last survivor in *The Masque of the Red Death*.

director, Nicolas Roeg, are suffused with red – violently contrasted with alternate rooms, whose décor is chiefly white, then yellow, then purple, then black, as the heroine runs through in terror, only to find her host apparently dead. Price's sardonic sadism flourishes in a world where horror is perpetrated not just to view the blood and pain, but also to see whether it has a value of its own above good and evil. When the Red Death strikes and Price stands alone, brooding above the fallen and blood-spattered revellers, Corman has come near to the last terrible sentence of Poe's tale: 'And Darkness and Decay and the Red Death held illimitable dominion over all'.

The worm and the decay that cause the death of the people inside the hall become the woodworm and wet rot in Poe's other tale of ruin, 'The Fall of the House of

More terrifying than all is Rackham's own image of the Red Death, come to hold its illimitable dominion over all.

The brooding Roderick Usher in Beardsley's drawing.

Usher'. There the writer and friend of Roderick Usher feels 'with the first glimpse of the building, a sense of insufferable gloom'. The house is built above the vapours and 'rank miasma' of a black tarn. Its hall is Gothic, its owner haunted and spectred, his twin sister 'the Lady Madeline' dying of a wasting disease that none can cure. Sure enough, she falls into a cataleptic trance and is buried too soon. Then, on a night of mist and lightning, her brother hears her come back from the family vault and shrieks to his friend.

'*We have put her living in the tomb!* Said I not that my senses were acute? I *now* tell you that I heard her first feeble movements in the hollow coffin. I heard them – many, many days ago – yet I dared not – *I dared not speak!* And now – tonight . . . will she not be here anon? Is she not hurrying to upbraid me for my haste? Have I not heard her footsteps on the stair? . . .

Madeline rises from the coffin in *The Fall of the House of Usher* of 1947.

In Corman's *The House of Usher*, Price is strangled by his sister, come back from the dead.

MADMAN! I TELL YOU THAT SHE NOW STANDS WITHOUT THE DOOR!'

She does stand there, the Lady Madeline, with blood on her white robes, emaciated and reeling. As her brother runs forwards, she clutches him and kills him in her own death-agony. Usher's friend flees aghast. And behind him, he sees in the wild lightnings and vaporous miasma and blood-red moon, the vast house of Usher split open and sink in the depths of the dark tarn.

The eerie, brooding presence of the tale has always attracted experimental filmmakers, more in love with suggestion than *grand guignol.* It was twice made in 1928 as an exercise in film, once by Jean Epstein and once by James Sibley White and Melville Webber. Epstein's film used slow motion and magical objects worthy of that film magician, Méliès. He even had Luis Buñuel as an assistant, before Buñuel made his own two masterpieces of surrealism, *Un Chien Andalou* and *L'Age d'Or.* The swamp sequences shot in the Sologne are very fine, but the Gothic studio effects of gusts of wind

nipping out candle flames, mists rising and blinds fluttering are rather overdone. Yet its portentousness was thistledown compared with the contemporary American version of *The Fall of the House of Usher.* That tried to do everything by mood and to exclude characters. It secured high praise from *avant-garde* American filmmakers, and forgot its audience. Hardly seen, it was much heard of in terms such as these from Padraic Colum in 'The Dial':

'*The Fall of the House of Usher* produced by the Film Guild develops from *The Cabinet of Dr. Caligari.* In that memorable photoplay the settings were made accessories to the story; they expressed the fantastic mood of the play. In *The Fall of the House of Usher* an experiment is made that goes further in this direction: the cast is of the smallest and the settings quite dominate the people in the film. What goes to establish the mood is the interior of the strange house, with its corridors and vaults, its dimly lighted rooms, its toppling walls and arches. Motion is given to things which should be inanimate and the strange shapes that fill

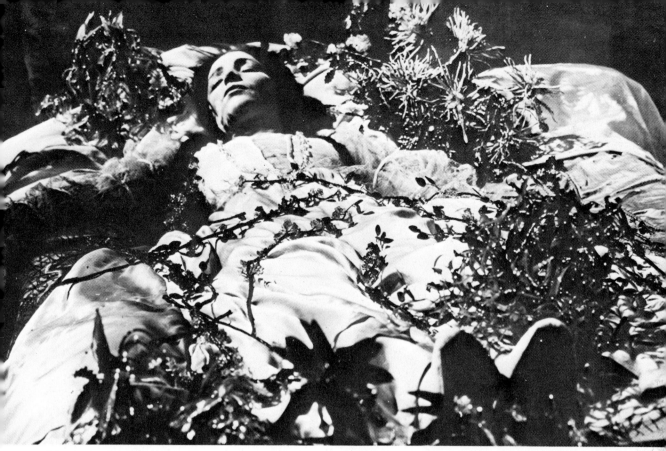

The Lady Madeline looks like Ophelia in Epstein's *La Chute de la Maison Usher* **of 1928 . . . before she is sealed in her coffin.**

the interior are made more sinister by this device . . . it is as if it was the expression, not of Poe's story, but of some music that accompanied that story.'

Once again, the subject of Usher attracted two young film-makers who were later to become professionals. The director of the 8-millimetre version of 1942 was Curtis Harrington, its young lead Anthony Perkins, who would seem good casting for Roderick Usher, except that Harrington himself played Roderick and Madeline Usher, both sides of the twin self.

The first full feature made of the subject was the British version of 1947, which has to be seen to be discredited. It opens to a prologue, which naïvely declares: 'Talking of horror stories, those of Edgar Allan Poe take quite a lot of beating'. It continues with a wooden showing of the tale that would be laughable, if it were not so dull. Its makers are best left fallen with the fragments of the House of Usher into the waters of the tarn and merciful oblivion.

The Corman version of *The Fall of the House of Usher* of 1960 launched him into

The House of Usher stands sinking above the tarn in Rackham's illustration. It is far more gothic and intense than the experimental films on the subject.

The sets dominate Dr. Caligari – but never to the exclusion of the characters.

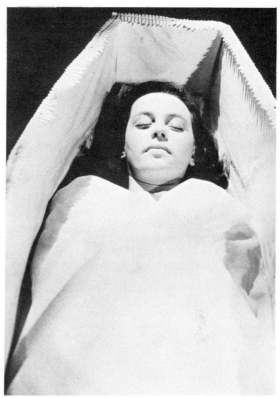

The Lady Madeline is sealed in her coffin in the British *House of Usher* of 1947.

his Poe cycle of films and did something to capture the haunted feeling of the original. In Richard Matheson's screenplay, the hero, played by Mark Damon, arrives at the house to see his betrothed, Madeline Usher. He is warned away by her brother Roderick, played by Vincent Price, who warns him that the Usher line should perish utterly and end its family history of strange madness. When Madeline falls into her catalepsy and is immured in her coffin, the hero discovers that her brother has *deliberately* buried her alive to end the Usher line. But the insane Madeline, now possessed with inhuman strength, escapes from her coffin to attack both her lover and her tormentor, Roderick. The house splits open and burns. A falling beam kills the last of the Ushers, as the hero escapes and the House sinks flaming into the pitchy waters. *(See Colour Section)*

Vincent Price's first performance in the Corman Poe-cycle has more to do with acting and less with his world-weary

Left: The cataleptic Madeline is buried alive in the family vault of Usher   *Below :* Her brother horrifies her lover with the grotesques of the house.

The demented Lady Madeline tries to kill lover . . . and brother.

Brother and sister are united in death as the blazing House of Usher falls.

persona than in his later appearances. He seems more controlled as Roderick Usher, and therefore more truly sinister. His compelling performance is helped by Floyd Crosby's creeping and atmospheric camera-work, as well as by the special effects of Ray Mercer. Although the budget is obviously small, the lighting and the sets are halfway to Poe's conception and Corman's true description of his film, in which he declared: 'The House is the Monster'.

So far, Poe's most Gothic and atmospheric film of *place* has not been made again. Yet its mood has influenced all the films of haunted houses that derive from the same tradition of 'The Monk' and 'The Mysteries of Udolpho'. *The Old Dark House* of 1932 and its many imitations, which always begin with the hero arriving in a storm at a forbidding mansion, all owe something to the House of Usher. It may have fallen and have been swallowed up in the black tarn, but its miasmic and troubled spirit haunts us yet. The House is the Monster.

Price in one of his best and most-controlled roles as Roderick Usher.

The hero escapes from the brooding atmosphere of Corman's *The House of Usher*.

The grisly gang meet in *The Old Dark House* and Poe-inspired gloom.

The Track of the Beast

'Poe invented the detective story in order that he might not go mad.'
Joseph Wood Krutch

'We know too much of life. We shall play a little game – a game of death, if you will . . .'
Karloff to Lugosi in The Black Cat *(1934)*

In his most famous detective story, 'The Murders in the Rue Morgue', Poe started two of the most enduring types of cinema – the sleuth film and the man-beast film. In Poe's version, the detective was the elegant and rational C. Auguste Dupin, the precursor of Sherlock Holmes and Hercule Poirot and a host of lesser imitators. His murderer was an orang-outang, brought to Paris by a sailor from Borneo; it managed to escape with its master's razor and kill two women most horribly in the Rue Morgue. Before Dupin gives a considered solution of the crime, Poe has had all the pleasure of describing the horrendous scene of bloodshed, as viewed by the sailor-owner of the beast:

'. . . The daughter lay prostrate and motionless; she had swooned. The screams and struggles of the old lady (during which the hair was torn from her head) had the effect of changing the probably pacific purposes of the orang-outang into those of wrath. With one determined sweep of its muscular arm it nearly severed her head from her body. The sight of blood inflamed its anger into frenzy. Gnashing its teeth, and flashing fire from its eyes, it flew upon the body of the girl, and imbedded its fearful talons in her throat, retaining its grasp until she expired. Its wandering and wild glances fell at this moment upon the head of the bed, over which the face of its master, rigid with horror, was just discernible. The fury of the beast, who no doubt bore still in mind the dreaded whip, was instantly converted into fear. Conscious of having deserved punishment, it seemed desirous of concealing its bloody deeds, and skipped about the chamber in an agony of nervous agitation; throwing down and breaking the furniture as it moved, and dragging the bed from the bedstead. In conclusion, it seized first the corpse of the daughter, and thrust it up the chimney, as it was found; then that of the old lady, which it immediately hurled through the window headlong . . . There lay the corpse of the old lady, with her throat so entirely cut that, upon attempt to raise her, the head fell off . . .'

As well as the description of the monstrous killer ape, which was to prefigure a whole minor branch of cinema and one masterpiece, *King Kong,* Poe presents the fastidious sleuth Dupin. This private detective, in his words, concentrates on 'the analysis of the *principles of* investigation'. He '*reasons* the matter throughout'. He is the superior of the police, who may be renowned for their cunning, but who lack method. When diligence and activity fail, they are baffled. They err constantly because of the intensity of their investigations. They need to hold back, to think, to solve the crime in the study from the collected evidence, not to scurry about gathering too many clues.

If Poe invented the detective story, his method was far too refined for the crudities of the thriller, just as his tales of mystery were far too subtle for the horror

Beardsley's orang-outang is curiously smooth and sinister as it carries the corpse of the daughter to stuff it up the chimney.

It is obvious from the laboratory and the poster cooked up for Lugosi that Carl Laemmle had *Frankenstein* in mind.

cinema. The four main versions of the film of 'The Murders in the Rue Morgue' show a greater emphasis on the bloodshed than on the unravelling of the crime. The first version, a silent film produced by Sol Rosenberg in 1914, left no print of the beast behind it, and no trace of its merits. The second was Robert Florey's version of 1932 when he had lost the direction of *Frankenstein* to James Whale. *The Murders in the Rue Morgue* was his consolation prize from Carl Laemmle of Universal, and he was assigned the great Karl Freund as his cameraman and Bela Lugosi as his star. Curiously enough, the young Bette Davis was dropped from the girl's part, or else the film might have achieved more of a reputation than it has.

The film does not deserve a cult. Its overtones of scabrous sex, in which Dr. Mirakle (played by Lugosi) gets his gorilla to abduct girls in order to breed bestially with them is shot as demurely as a croquet party. The best sequences are those in which Lugosi mocks his caged ape. Yet the moment that the ape gets out and begins to menace the

The gorilla courts his victim as bashfully as if it were his first date.

Lugosi mocks his ape.

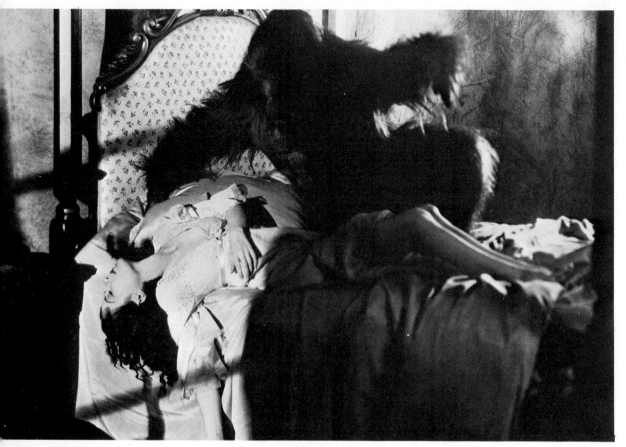

The ape menaces the girl.

victim virgins, it reveals itself to be a sad actor called Charlie Gomorra capering about in a monkey suit. While Lugosi gets his deserts in the end and is strangled by his hairy evil-doer, yet even Freund's expressionist camera work cannot save this Poe vehicle from being risible. As for the subtleties of detection, the sleuthing is done by a love-lorn medical student and the script written by authors wearing boxing-gloves – even though some of the dialogue is credited to John Huston.

The third version of the film was made in 1954 by Roy del Ruth in 3-D and Technicolor to emphasise the gory details. It starred Karl Malden as an insane zoologist, before he rose to fame as the voyeuristic husband in *Baby Doll*. He used a man-gorilla controlled by hypnosis to kill women in Paris. Although the director and the teaser-advertising manipulated the threat of the hairy paw to grope above the

The ape throttles its master, Lugosi.

Karl Malden shows the gorilla escaped from its cage in the 1954 *Phantom of the Rue Morgue*.

audience in 3-D and to menace passers-by in the posters, the film was messy and simplistic. The threat of bestial rape was exaggerated at the expense of Poe's prose and the result was predictably dull.

Gordon Hessler filmed the fourth version of Poe's tale in Spain in 1971. He starred Herbert Lom playing a disfigured man, who is seeking revenge against Jason Robards, the owner of a *grand guignol* theatre, in which he is 'beheaded' nightly by an axe-wielding 'ape'. The love interest is provided by Christine Kaufmann, while Lilli Palmer also makes a brief come-back. While arguably the best of the versions of *The Murders in the Rue Morgue*, it is still as far from the eerie suggestibility and subtlety of Poe as Hollywood Boulevard is from the Boul' Mich'. It has, however, interesting echoes of another Poe obsession, 'The Premature Burial', and has the

Below and over page: **Teaser posters show how Poe's name and concept were used to lure in the audiences to see the remakes of his story.**

CAN IT BE HUMAN?

"PHANTOM OF THE RUE MORGUE"

disfigured Lom return from the dead through a carnival stunt.

Poe's second most famous detective story, 'The Mystery of Marie Rogêt', was only filmed once because it imposed the intellectual rigours and *longueurs* of a rational solution onto the processes of film-making, where screen-time is three times as fast as theatre time and even faster in terms of everyday life. Phil Rosen was the director, and his screen-writer tried to keep to the convolutions of Poe's efforts to solve the mystery of the actual girl found drowned in the Seine. Yet though faithful to Poe, the film is unfaithful to the cinema, choosing a wearisome plot that not even the fires of Maria Montez as the victim can stoke up. She is at least allowed to play herself as a comedy star and to be resurrected – it was

not her body in the Seine, after all.

Poe's most original and distinguished detective story, starring C. Auguste Dupin, 'The Purloined Letter', was never filmed, as it is too short even to bulk out. But two other sleuthing stories of his, 'The Gold-Bug' and 'Maelzel's Chess-Player', have had their directors. 'The Gold-Bug' with its complicated cryptographic plot revolving round a burnished Egyptian scarab-beetle was made in a derisory American version under the title of *Manfish* in 1956 and as a French short film by Robert Lachenung in 1960. 'Maelzel's Chess-Player', in which Poe demonstrated his extraordinary powers of reasoning as early as 1836, exposed a famous Automaton Chess-Player as a hoax, run by a dwarf in a series of boxes, which opened in turn, but allowed him to pass from one to the other ahead of possible discovery. It was unfortunately destroyed before Poe's hypothesis about it could be checked; but Poe's sketch of the mechanical Turk playing his game above his boxes still exists.

French directors made 'The Chess-Player' twice in 1926 and 1938, the second time starring Conrad Veidt, the Lon Chaney of the European horror cinema with a career stretching from *Dr. Caligari* for twenty years until the Second World War. What Poe had done was to link an obsession with the mechanics of chess with an obsession with death, so that the first great chess game

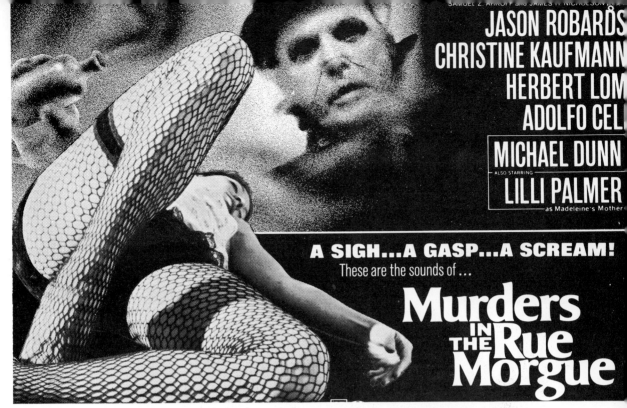

A SIGH...A GASP...A SCREAM!
These are the sounds of ...

Murders IN THE Rue Morgue

The two teaser posters of the 1971 remake were far more sexually explicit. They have the heroine with spread legs openly menaced by both gorilla's paw and vitriol bottle.

Edgar Allan Poe's
masterpiece of
the grotesque...

Murders in the Rue Morgue

Lugosi tries to avoid defeat by Karloff in *The Black Cat* (1934).

in the cinema is played in Ulmer's *The Black Cat* of 1934, so distant from Poe's plots, so near to Poe's moods. In that game, Lugosi has lost his wife and daughter to the Satanist Karloff, and now plays for his girl-companion – and loses. As Karloff says in his most macabre way, 'We know too much of life. We shall play a little game – a game of death if you will . . .' The echo of this chess-game was picked up by Bergman in *The Seventh Seal,* where the knight cheats Death by knocking

Poe's sketch of Maelzel's chess-player appears in his story about a solution to the problem of the Automaton.

The Knight also tries not to lose to Death in *The Seventh Seal* (1956).

Albert Finney plays Hercule Poirot (Agatha Christie's version of C. Auguste Dupin) with a train-load of stars in the old-fashioned *Murder on the Orient Express* **(1974).**

over the pieces and saving the lives of the Clown, his Wife and the Child.

Yet Poe's detective heirs fill the screen. If the tradition of the long final explanation invented by him – used most memorably by Bogart in *The Maltese Falcon* and most recently by Finney in *Murder on the Orient Express* – is now outdated, yet the cool sleuth, two jumps ahead of the police and one jump ahead of the criminal, has entertained us since the beginning of the movies.

It may seem a far cry from the Southern-gentleman Poe to *Shaft's Big Score,* but the lone all-powerful gumshoe is still based on the product of Poe's drugged and logical and fastidious and deranged and paranoiac mind.

Shaft is yet another lone sleuth rooting out all evil, as he blasts away at the enemy by this gothic tombstone.

The Haunted Palace

'I have reached these lands but newly
*   From an ultimate dim Thule —*
From a wild weird clime that lieth, sublime
*   Out of SPACE — out of TIME.'*
From Poe's 'Dreamland'.

Poe once wrote a poem called 'The Haunted Palace'. There a monarch lived in the greenest of valleys; but evil things in robes of sorrow surrounded him, and he died. Vast forms now move beyond the red-lit windows of his palace; strange sounds come from it; but harmony and joy have fled. And the hideous throng that comes out of the pale door of the palace laughs — yet smiles no more.

Poe wrote another poem about a haunted place, 'The City in the Sea'. It lay toward the dim West, it was the drowned throne of Death with time-eaten towers:

> *'. . . Light from out the lurid sea*
> *Streams up the turrets silently —*
> *Gleams up the pinnacles far and free —*
> *Up domes — up spires — up kingly halls —*
> *Up fanes — up Babylon-like walls . . .*
> *Resignedly beneath the sky*
> *The melancholy waters lie.*
> *So blend the turrets and shadows there*
> *That all seem pendulous in air,*
> *While from a proud tower in the town*
> *Death looks gigantically down.'*

To haunted palace and lurid drowned city, Poe added a third nightmare, a dream-land where the Ghouls lived in an ultimate Thule. It was haunted by ill angels, while on a black throne, an Eilodon reigned, named NIGHT. Poe claimed to have reached these dark illimitable lands but newly —

> *From a wild weird clime that lieth, sublime*
> *Out of SPACE — out of TIME.*

Such dark visions haunted Poe and have prowled down the corridors of the mind of Gothic directors ever since. When Roger Corman seemed to have come to the bottom of Poe's maelstrom, he called a film of his 'The Haunted Palace' and took as his inspiration Poe's poem. The plot deals with a warlock in New England in 1765, who raises people from the dead by magic rites discovered in a book of black magic called the 'Necronomicon'. He is burned alive as a warlock and vows to rise again from the dead — which he seems to do a century later. His identical descendent takes over his old house, which has become 'The Haunted Palace' of the poem and is inhabited by deformed adults and children. These prove to be the weird offspring of humans and those 'evil things, in robes of sorrow', which Poe had described, although they look more like the mutants of the atomic age that Corman used to film before he became Poe-obsessed. In the film, the villagers once again mass to attack the new warlock — increasingly possessed by the old one — and they finally burn down the haunted palace. But the warlock escapes again . . .

All run-of-the-mill horror stuff, using Poe's name like an incantation to add class to what is crass. Yet the posters were titillating and starred Poe's name almost in the same size as Vincent Price's. The blood-curdling first film of Corman's assistant, Francis Ford Coppola — later to become more famous than his teacher — was titled in English, *The Haunted and the Hunted* and was also a tale of a ghostly Irish

W. Heath Robinson illustrated the evil spirits
pulling down the monarch in 'The Haunted
Palace'. He also drew a head-piece for 'The
City in the Sea', and an illustration for Night
on its throne for 'Dreamland'.

Vincent Price raises the dead as a warlock in *The Haunted Palace* (1967). The script was also influenced by a story of Lovecraft, 'The Case of Charles Dexter Ward'.

Warlock Price is burned at the stake.

The deformed mutants meet the appalled
descendents of the first warlock. . . and haunt the
stairs of the 'Palace'.

Price and his wife fight possession by the old
warlock and his woman . . . but the dead come
back.

mansion named Castlehalora. (In America, its title was *Dementia 13* and its series of axe-murders probably qualify the young Coppola as the perpetrator of more rolling heads than anyone since Monsieur Guillotine in the Days of the Terror in the French Revolution.) Yet even the English title was taken at second-hand, less from Poe's poem than from another earlier Vincent Price vehicle, directed and produced by William Castle, who knew that a Haunted House was the traditional mass attraction in those fairgrounds from which the magic cinema of Méliès originally had sprung.

Corman and his followers did not have anything to do with the last remaining feature film which used Poe's name with Vincent Price's to capitalise on the dying Poe movie craze in 1965. This was the British *City Under the Sea*, sometimes entitled *War-Gods of the Deep*. Its director was almost as historical as his subject – Jacques Tourneur, the son of the legendary Maurice Tourneur, who had made Poe's 'The System of Dr. Tarr and Professor Fether' in France in 1912 and had then exported the horror film to America when he had been sent to run the Eclair studio in the United States. His son had directed *Cat People* for Val Lewton in the 1940s, and

William Castle's gothic Price picture dated back to 1958.

The gillman plunging towards the sunken city has an unknown poster artist almost worthy of Rackham himself.

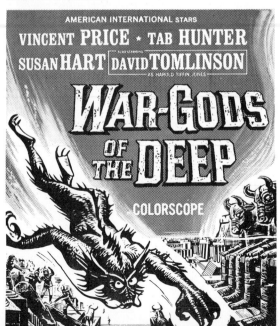

The diving-gear of the humans is rather lumpish compared with the gillman's plunge.

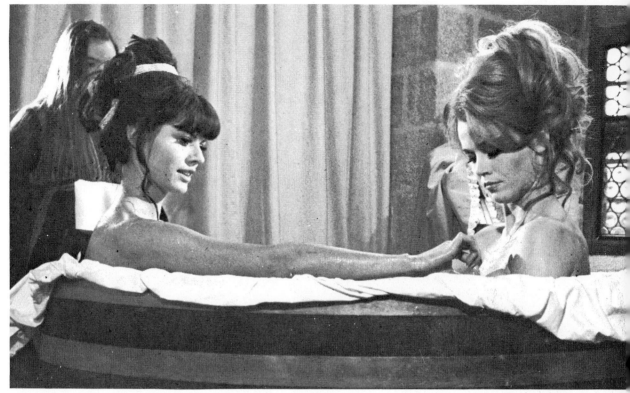

Jane Fonda enjoys a bath with her maid in *Metzengerstein* . . .

thus he was a fitting director to make one of the last of the Poe films after Corman's eight-in-a-row.

The film is concerned with a fishy gillman (looking very like *The Creature from the Black Lagoon*), which comes from the submerged city of Lyonesse off Cornwall. The hero and heroine tumble there through a Poe-like Maelstrom, to find themselves in a weird undersea hall, lit by the lurid fires of sunken volcanoes, and ornamented by bull-headed Egyptian statues that seem to have more to do with Karnak than Atlantis or Camelot. Prisoners, who disobey the mad Captain who rules Lyonesse, are fed to the carnivorous gillmen. Yet somehow, the hero and heroine win a seabed chase and escape out of a sunken cavern toward the sun, which destroys the mad Captain.

Although Poe's poems inspired directly no more features – and even indirectly 'Dreamland' could hardly be held responsible for such psychedelic disasters as *The Trip* – one more fascinating compilation movie was made in 1968 out of three of Poe's tales, 'William Wilson', 'Toby Dammit', and 'Metzengerstein'. Each tale was directed by a different name director – Malle, Fellini and Vadim. The result was not successful, when it was released under the title of *Spirits of the Dead* or *Tales of Mystery*. Malle's 'William Wilson' has been treated earlier in this book; but Fellini's 'Toby Dammit' received high critical praise. Fellini largely ignored Poe to enter his own private world of bizarre images; but by casting Terence Stamp as a fading, self-pitying matinée idol, doomed to a last death-ride in his red Maserati, Fellini cut away the facade and pretensions of the film world of Rome, ending on a shot of a small child picking up a severed head.

Yet if Fellini gave a dazzling display in 'Toby Dammit', Vadim shamelessly misused Poe's terrible story of the mythical death-horse in 'Metzengerstein' as a vehicle for his wife of the time, Jane Fonda, and his own bizarre tastes. Miss Fonda appears in a succession of costumes that seem left over

She joins in a threesome with the maid and her lover . . .

She joins now in a threesome with her brother and her horse.

from a medieval Barbarella and plays a debauched countess in love with her brother, whom she burns to death, but who returns as a black stallion to rape her to her death. As the brother's role was actually played by Peter Fonda, the theme of incest seemed real enough, as did the lesbianism of a bath sequence and the bestiality of Miss Fonda's passion for horses.

Edgar Allan Poe can hardly be blamed for the misuse film-makers, great and little, have made of him. He might wish like Prince Metzengerstein himself to leap upon his fiery demon nightmare and ride over the Gothic turrets and celluloid crenelations of his self-loving copyists and whirl them to their flaming deaths in the conflagration of their own petty constructions, lit from the holocaust of his wild imagination.

Yet the true eerie feeling of the demon horse and girl is caught better in a French postcard of 1900.

Rackham brilliantly captures the castle ending in flames with the demon horse riding above.

Himself the Undead

'Man doth not yield him to the angels, nor unto death utterly, *save only through the weakness of his feeble will.'*
From Poe's 'Ligeia'.

Although the cinema owes much to Edgar Allan Poe, it has paid him little direct homage by masterworks shot under his name. As his most intelligent critic so far, Pierre Gires, has written, Poe's black sense of humour and science-fiction writing have much influenced film-makers and other writers without their acknowledgement of

This teaser from the Press-book of the 1971 *Murders in the Rue Morgue* shows the use of Poe (and Rackham's drawings) in the campaign for a film that bears little literary or pictorial resemblance to the originators of the story.

"...and much of madness and more of sin... and horror the soul of the plot." —EDGAR ALLAN POE 1839

Edgar Allan Poe's masterpiece of the grotesque...

Murders IN THE Rue Morgue

GP

their source. Poe first described a voyage to the moon well before Verne or Wells in his version of the marvellous adventure of Hans Pfaall, who got to the moon by balloon, only to find it full of exploding volcanoes and little people without ears. Méliès used a similar route to the moon, but through Verne. Poe also foretold the end of the world by a collision between the Earth and a comet in his Conversation of Eiros with Charmion – a solution which Abel Gance took for his film, *The End of the World*. It was also Poe who popularised the principal themes of Reincarnation, the Alter Ego, Hypnotism, the Phantom Vessel, the Devil in Human Shape the Confession through Remorse, the Plague, Claustrophobia, the Doomed House, the Avenging Beast, and the Death-in-Life of the Loved Woman. As for the theme of Reincarnation alone – along with the Egyptian influence shown in 'The Gold-Bug' and the 'Small Discussion with a Mummy' and 'The Black Cat' – the series of films on Mummys coming back to life owe much to the bandages wrapped round Poe's corpse.

There is no question that the works of all the great magic and Gothic film-makers from Méliès to Bergman, from Buñuel to Corman would not have been the same without the wide reading of Poe in the late nineteenth and early twentieth century. If Corman was the director most identified immediately with Poe, he will be remembered best for his capture of the gallows humour in Poe, whose plots he otherwise shamefully misused to parade his actors' talents. His own burlesque of all his Poe

Mélies' magic voyages to the moon are by shell, balloon-train, or coach – whatever way they take, his travellers get there – and the moon-men are weird enough for Poe himself.

In Gance's *The End of the World* (1930) an orgy takes place on Earth as it does in 'The Masque of the Red Death', knowing that no one may survive.

Murnau makes his Dracula arrive at Whitby on a Phantom Ship – a concept partly taken by Bram Stoker from Poe's 'Manuscript Found in a Bottle'.

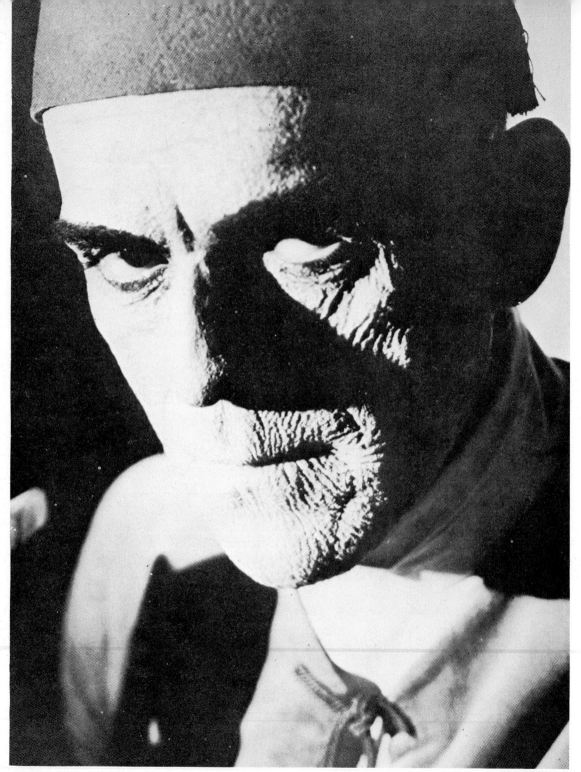

The Mummy, **played by Boris Karloff in 1932.**

films, *The Comedy of Terrors* of 1963, was in many ways truest to Poe's sense of mockery, although it was the only one of Corman's Gothic extravaganzas not credited to Poe. It also reunited the four masters of world-weary Poe black humour, Price and Karloff, Lorre and Rathbone, with even Joe E.

Brown making a cemetery appearance to show his mouth as wide as an open grave.

Poe loved the perverse. In his story, 'The Imp of the Perverse,' he told of a man forced to confess a crime from the sheer itch of wanting to show how clever he was, wanting his glorification in his own down-

The Comedy of Terrors re-united in a requiem farce the masters of Corman's Poe films.

Karloff and Lugosi are the true actors of Poe in *The Black Cat* (1934).

The victim screams under the gargoyle in _The Masque of the Red Death_ (1964).

fall. Therefore, perversely, Poe may be taking pleasure in his after-life (if he has one) to find that those closest to his spirit are those who strayed furthest from his text. Ulmer's _The Black Cat_ remains the film most imbued in the mocking, macabre horror of Poe – yet it has little to do with Poe's original story. The avenging beasts of the title are more surely Lugosi and Karloff than household pets. The actual reciting of the poem of 'The Raven' by the lugubrious Lugosi in the film of that name of 1935 is ludicrous in its accuracy, while Corman's best Poe film, _The Masque of the Red Death,_ is closest to his master when he gives way to baroque personifications of Death and its messengers, not to be found in the original. It is actually perversely true that there are no versions of 'The Fall of the House of Usher' that so eerily capture Poe's miasma of claustrophobia and vengeance as well as the British _Dead of Night,_ when a country-house party plays out its murderous fantasies to their end.

Yet the perversity in Poe's nature that may have made him appreciate that his

The victim screams as she sees her death in the mirror in _Dead of Night_ (1943).

influence may have been greatest where it was most indirect, would not have led him to revel in the 'camp' absurdities of the furthest extents of his myths. Both Tarzan and Batman did not entirely escape the threat of the 'Tales of Mystery and Imagination'. Johnny Weissmuller even found himself faced with the wooden claw of Aquanetta, the Leopard Woman, while Batman and Robin were within a scratch of their lives from the Cat-Woman. From 'The Black Cat' to the serial and the comic strip may seem to be the descent of Poe himself into the maelstrom of the masses. But he has remained ever-popular, ever-black, ever-read, evermore. His presence, recognised and invisible, acknowledged and ignored, haunts our minds and our screens. He is himself the undead. He lies beyond the grave in the dying words of Ligeia: 'Who – who knoweth the mysteries of the will with its vigour? Man doth not yield him to the angels, *nor unto death utterly,* save only through the weakness of his feeble will.'